US NAVY PACIFIC FLEET
1941

America's mighty last battleship fleet

Mark Lardas
Illustrated by Edouard A. Groult

OSPREY PUBLISHING
Bloomsbury Publishing Plc
Kemp House, Chawley Park, Cumnor Hill, Oxford OX2 9PH, UK
29 Earlsfort Terrace, Dublin 2, Ireland
1385 Broadway, 5th Floor, New York, NY 10018, USA
E-mail: info@ospreypublishing.com
www.ospreypublishing.com

OSPREY is a trademark of Osprey Publishing Ltd

First published in Great Britain in 2024

A catalog record for this book is available from the British Library.

ISBN: PB 9781472859501; eBook 9781472859488; ePDF 9781472859518; XML 9781472859495

24 25 26 27 28   10 9 8 7 6 5 4 3 2 1

Maps by bounford.com
Diagrams by Adam Tooby
Index by Zoe Ross
Typeset by PDQ
Printed and bound in India by Replika Press Private Ltd.

Front Cover: Art by Edouard A. Groult, © Osprey Publishing
Osprey Publishing supports the Woodland Trust, the UK's leading woodland conservation charity.

To find out more about our authors and books visit www.ospreypublishing.com. Here you will find extracts, author interviews, details of forthcoming events and the option to sign up for our newsletter.

Author's Note:
The following abbreviations indicate the sources of the photographs used in this volume:
NARA – National Archives
USNHHC – United States Navy Heritage and History Command
Other sources are listed in full.

Author's Dedication:
To the memory of Professor Harry Bell Benford. He was a professor of Naval Architecture and Marine Engineering (NAME) at the University of Michigan when I attended. His Career Day presentation when I was a senior in high school led me to majoring in NAME at Michigan. He was as accomplished an author as he was a naval architect, who insisted his students learn to write well. While I wandered away from naval architecture, I still carry his lessons in technical writing with me today.

GLOSSARY
AV   series of seaplane tenders operated from the 1920s to the Vietnam War
AVP   small seaplane tender
AVD   seaplane tender, destroyer

CONTENTS

THE FLEET'S PURPOSE

When the US Pacific Fleet was created, its purpose was deterring war with Japan, to awe Japan into remaining at peace. It failed that task decisively. Some, including Admiral James O. Richardson, who commanded the Pacific Fleet's immediate predecessor, maintained that US Pacific Fleet's presence in Hawaii made war inevitable.

A secondary purpose was, in the event of war with Japan, to give the United States the capability to take the war from the United States' Pacific Coast to the Japanese Home Islands. It was intended to permit the United States to project power across over 5,000 miles of the earth's largest ocean. Within a year of the war's opening, the Pacific Fleet had begun that job. But the Pacific Fleet of 1942 was a different fleet from the 1941 Pacific Fleet, with different doctrines, different leaders, and many different ships and sailors.

In 1922, the United States Navy was reorganized into one fleet: the United States Fleet. There were several independent formations, such as the Asiatic Fleet, the Special Service Squadron (in the Caribbean) and US Naval Forces, Europe, but these were minor. Most of the US Navy's surface forces were intended to be used as a single unit in the event of a war, including all the battleships and most recent-construction cruisers and destroyers.

This followed the naval strategies of Alfred Thayer Mahan. He asserted that control of the sea was achieved by defeating the enemy's fleet in a decisive battle. This meant concentrating a navy into one force, especially the battle line, to guarantee victory in battles. Mahan (and US Navy planners) envisioned a navy fighting one major foe at a time, even against a coalition.

The single battle fleet concept resulted in formation of the United States Fleet. It was broken into a Battle Force, containing the battleships and supporting cruisers and destroyers, and a cruiser force, with the remaining cruisers and submarines in the Scouting Force. Its task was to seek out and find the enemy, and guide the Battle Force to engage it.

The US Pacific Fleet was created when the Navy split the US Fleet into independent parts due to the war in Europe. The portion of the US Fleet stationed in Hawaii (shown here in 1940), had the newest battleships and the biggest fleet aircraft carriers. (USNHHC)

The Navy stationed one force on each coast, with the two forces joining annually in either the Atlantic or Pacific for joint maneuvers. The split simplified peacetime logistics, keeping ports on both coasts active. In wartime, the fleet would unite against a foe. Notionally, this was the Japanese in the Pacific and the Royal Navy in the Atlantic. (No one seriously expected war with Britain, but through 1935 there was no other serious naval rival in the Atlantic and war plans had to use *someone* as the bad guy.)

Nazi Germany's emergence in 1933 eliminated the assumption that the US would fight just one major war with one major power. Germany's late-1930s rearmament and the start of World War II, when Germany invaded Poland, strengthened that belief. The fall of France in 1940 and Britain's continuation of the war left US President Franklin Roosevelt determined to enter the war as a British ally.

Roosevelt lacked the public support to declare war on Germany and Italy. Instead he assisted Britain in many ways short of war. This included maintaining a presence in the Atlantic, although the US still needed a strong fleet in the Pacific. Japan was becoming more belligerent as World War II continued, and the solution was to split the US Fleet into an Atlantic Fleet and a Pacific Fleet. The majority of the battleships and cruisers, along with three of the four large aircraft carriers, became the Pacific Fleet, while the oldest battleships and smaller carriers were assigned to the Atlantic Fleet.

The change was announced on February 1, 1941, taking effect the next day. Admiral James O. Richardson, who commanded the United States Fleet, was relieved of command. To replace him, Roosevelt named Rear Admiral Husband E. Kimmel to lead the new Pacific Fleet.

The US Pacific Fleet was a product of naval limitations treaties. The design of the heavy cruisers leading the formation came out of the Washington Treaty. Their categorization and the light cruiser in the rear were from the 1930 London Treaty. (USNHHC)

The 1941 United States Pacific Fleet was a product of three naval limitations treaties: the 1922 Washington Naval Treaty, the 1930 London Naval Treaty and the 1936 Second London Naval Treaty. Virtually all ships of the fleet were designed and built or modified under the terms of those three treaties. Warships predating those treaties were retained under their limitations. Although the Second London Treaty essentially lapsed in 1938, none of the new construction built after that was then in the Pacific Fleet.

The Washington Treaty limited the number of each navy's battleships (15 each for the Royal Navy and US Navy, nine for the Japanese). It halted future battleship construction for ten years, and assigned each navy an aggregate tonnage limit for aircraft carriers and battleships. The maximum tonnage for battleships was set at 35,000 tons and aircraft carriers at 27,000 tons (with exceptions for aircraft carriers converted from dreadnoughts). It also limited all other warships to maximum tonnage of 10,000 tons, with guns no larger than 8in. (including aircraft carrier guns). It forbade Britain, Japan and the United States from constructing new Pacific fortifications.

While ending a battleship-building race, the Washington Treaty triggered a cruiser- and destroyer-building race. This led to the 1930 London Naval Treaty, which differentiated between cruisers with an 8in. battery (heavy cruisers) and those with 6.1in. and smaller main guns (light cruisers). It limited the maximum displacement of destroyers and submarines, the numbers of heavy cruisers each navy could possess, and provided an aggregate limit in tonnage for cruisers, destroyers and submarines. It also provided unlimited tonnage of warships between 600 and 2,000 tons with a maximum speed no greater than 20 knots, no torpedo tubes and no more than four gun mounts for guns greater than 3in. and less than 6.1in.

This was followed by the Second London Treaty in 1936, which attempted to constrain new battleship construction and further limit cruiser and submarine maximum sizes. Japan refused to sign, so within two years it was disregarded.

These three treaties shaped the ships available to the Pacific Fleet in 1941. The 1934 Vinson-Trammell Act let the US Navy build up to the allowable limits of the Washington and 1930 London Treaties. Its fruits populated the 1941 Pacific Fleet. The Naval Act of 1938 expanded the Navy's size slightly by 1941, but not until the 1940 Two-Ocean Navy (or Vinson-Walsh) Act was signed in July 1940 did the Navy expand significantly. None of that construction was available to the Pacific Fleet in 1941. If it went to war, it went with ships built under the naval limitations treaties.

FLEET FIGHTING POWER

THE SHIPS

In 1941, the US Pacific Fleet had five categories of major warships: battleships, aircraft carriers, cruisers, destroyers and submarines. It possessed auxiliary warships, primarily mine warfare vessels of various types, and it had a fleet train, fleet auxiliaries allowing extended operations at distances far from the Pacific Fleet's main bases. On December 7, 1941, the Pacific fleet numbered 108 major warships, 22 auxiliary warships and 55 fleet auxiliaries.

There were also 68 warships, auxiliary warships and fleet auxiliaries assigned to the naval districts controlling the bases from which the Pacific Fleet operated. These included gunboats, older destroyers, mine warfare vessels, tenders and auxiliaries. Sixteen were stationed at Pearl Harbor's 14th Naval District. While not part of the Pacific Fleet, they could be drawn upon.

Battleships

When the Pacific Fleet was created, it had 12 battleships, two each of the Oklahoma, Pennsylvania and California classes and three each of the New Mexico and Colorado classes. They represented four-fifths of the US Navy's available battleships and were widely viewed as the US Navy's main offensive punch.

They were divided into three-ship divisions. The Colorados and New Mexicos were in homogeneous divisions. One Nevada-class battleship belonged to the

Oklahoma was the second-oldest battleship in the Pacific Fleet and the only one with reciprocating engines. Scheduled to be retired in May 1942 and refloated after being sunk at Pearl Harbor, it was not returned to service. (USNHHC)

divisions made up of the two-battleship Pennsylvania and California classes. Intended to fight as a 12-ship squadron, until the two North Carolina-class battleships were commissioned in late 1941, these were the most modern battleships in the US Navy.

US Navy leaders believed them superior in force to the battleships possessed by Japan. Four Japanese battleships were built as battle cruisers, but one of those was presumed demilitarized. The remaining US Navy battleships, all commissioned prior to World War I, were relegated to the secondary Atlantic where their limitations would not hold back the Pacific Fleet. However, the Pacific Fleet would not retain this superiority long.

Conditions in the Atlantic deteriorated during 1941. The Commander-in-Chief of the Navy transferred the 3rd Battle Division, with three New Mexico-class battleships, to the Atlantic. This left the Pacific Fleet inferior to Japan with nine battleships to ten. The four Japanese battlecruisers had been rebuilt as fast battleships, including the previously demilitarized *Hiei*, and the Japanese battleships were faster than the Pacific Fleet's battle line. Yet in 1941, Pacific Fleet commanders still believed their battle line allowed them to take the war to Japan.

All Pacific Fleet battleships carried a main battery of 14in. or 16in. guns, a secondary battery of casemate 5in. guns and a 5in. antiaircraft battery. By 1941, none had torpedo tubes; they had been removed from the ones which carried them when built. All except the oldest pair had a top speed of 21 knots and the Nevada class could reach 20 knots. All were designed as oil-fired vessels, and all were propelled by steam turbines, except *Oklahoma*, with triple-expansion reciprocating steam engines.

The oldest pair, *Nevada* and *Oklahoma*, made up the Nevada class. Transitional warships, second-generation "superdreadnoughts", they were the second class of US dreadnoughts to be armed with 14in. guns, in this case the 14in./45cal. They were the first to carry 14in. guns in triple turrets and the last to carry 14in. guns in twin turrets, carrying their main battery in two triple turrets and two superfiring twin turrets. *Nevada* was the first battleship since the Delaware class with steam turbines; *Oklahoma* the last equipped with reciprocating steam engines. They were the first US battleships designed with oil-fired boilers, fuel used on all subsequent battleships.

They were the first US battleships to use "all-or-nothing" armor. A single deep-armor 13.5in. belt covered the most vital parts of the ships (machinery, magazines, turret mechanisms and conning tower), with even thicker armor on the turrets and barbettes. The superstructure, bow and stern were largely unarmored, although the propeller shafts were protected by armor roughly 40 percent as thick as the main belt. They had 6in. of deck armor over the citadel, split into upper and lower armored deck.

The price paid for the heavy armor and battery was speed. Their engines could only reach 20.5 knots. Following several rebuilds, these ships displaced 29,000 tons in a hull 583ft long and 108ft wide. Theirs was the pattern used in all subsequent US Navy battleships.

The follow-on Pennsylvania class, *Pennsylvania* and *Arizona*, were Nevada upgrades. They were 608ft long, with a 106ft beam. With a mean draft of 28ft, they drew half a foot more depth than the Nevadas, and had a standard displacement of 33,100 tons. They used the same 14in./45cal main guns as their predecessors, carrying 12in. four triple turrets. Their main belt armor was half an inch thicker and their two armored decks totaled 6in. They also had four propellers to the Nevadas' two. They were slightly faster, with a top speed of 21 knots, probably due to their better length-to-beam ratio and engines that were 30 percent more powerful.

The three New Mexico-class battleships, *New Mexico*, *Idaho* and *Mississippi*, were near-copies of the Pennsylvanias. They had the same main gun arrangement, same displacement, same speed and same belt armor. There were differences: they mounted 12 14in./50cal guns, which were more powerful with greater range than the earlier 14in./45cal guns. They also had a clipper bow to improve seakeeping. This increased overall length to 624ft, although waterline length remained the same. They also had thicker deck armor, 10in. Finally, they used turbo-electric drive, where steam turbines powered electric motors that drove the four propeller shafts.

West Virginia was the newest battleship in the Pacific Fleet in 1941, the culmination of US second-generation battleship design. Sunk at Pearl Harbor, it was refloated, refitted and returned to combat. This photo shows it in 1939. (NARA)

The two California-class ships, *California* and *Tennessee,* were similarly developments of the New Mexicos. They repeated the preceding class's main gun arrangement and turbo-mechanical drive. Laid down after the Battle of Jutland in 1916, their main difference from the preceding class was better damage control arrangements. They also reverted to the 6in. horizontal armor of the Pennsylvania class, and were 1,000 tons lighter than the New Mexicos. They were the first US Navy battleships built with no casemate guns on the main deck.

The final class of battleships in the 1941 Pacific Fleet was the Maryland class: *Maryland, Colorado* and *West Virginia.* They were identical in almost every particular to the Californias, except in main battery. Instead of 14in. guns, they carried a 16in./45cal main battery; eight in four twin turrets. Although they had two-thirds the number of guns of the preceding classes, they had a broadside weight as great as the 12-gun 14in. battleships mounting 14in./50cal guns, and were 6 percent heavier than those carrying 14in./45cal guns.

Although the final Maryland-class battleship was not completed until 1923, the basic design predated World War I. The Pennsylvania class was authorized in 1912, and construction started in 1913. All subsequent designs were modifications of those ships. At the time, other dreadnoughts and torpedo boats were the greatest threats they were believed to face. Submarines were not then viewed as a serious threat to capital ships and military aircraft were mere powered box kites. Little thought was given to aerial threats or underwater protection.

By 1918, the submarine threat was clear. Aircraft were still fragile, but were already capable of damaging battleships. By then, battleship designs were locked

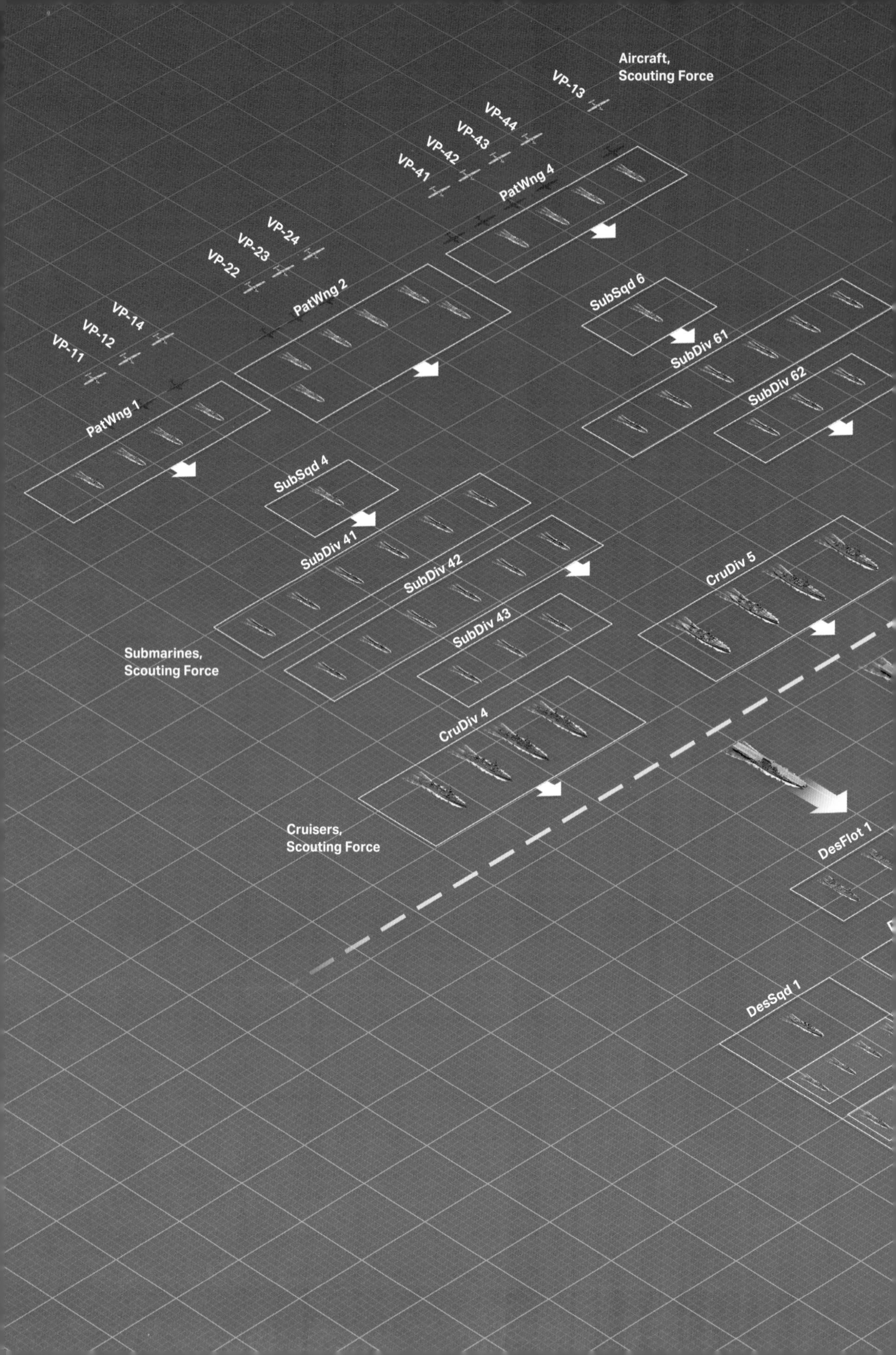

Aircraft,
Scouting Force

VP-13

VP-44

VP-43

VP-42

VP-41

PatWng 4

VP-24

VP-23

VP-22

PatWng 2

SubSqd 6

SubDiv 61

SubDiv 62

VP-14

VP-12

VP-11

PatWng 1

SubSqd 4

SubDiv 41

SubDiv 42

SubDiv 43

CruDiv 5

Submarines,
Scouting Force

CruDiv 4

Cruisers,
Scouting Force

DesFlot 1

DesSqd 1

THE US PACIFIC FLEET, 1941

Aircraft Carriers,
Battle Force

Destroyers,
Battle Force

DesFlot 2

DesSqd 6

Battle Force

DesSqd 4

CruDiv3

DesSqd 5

BatDiv 1

BatDiv 2

BatDiv 4

THE US PACIFIC FLEET, 1941 (previous pages)

In 1941, the Pacific Fleet was divided into two main parts: Battle Force with the battleships, aircraft carriers and light cruisers, and Scouting Force, comprising the fleet's heavy cruisers, submarines and long-range patrol aircraft. There was also Base Force, with the Pacific Fleet's auxiliary train, but only its seagoing tugs and fleet oilers routinely operated outside a harbor.

The heart of the US Pacific Fleet in 1941 was the battle line, consisting of the Battle Force battleship and cruiser divisions. In a surface action, as shown in the diagram, the battleships would be in the middle, with a cruiser division before and behind them. This allowed the cruisers to shield the battleship from torpedo attack without blocking its broadside fire. Light cruisers were used. Their 6in. guns had a high rate of fire, with shells capable of crippling any vessel launching a torpedo attack at a range great enough to engage outside torpedo range.

Destroyers, Battle Force broke down into five destroyer squadrons split between two destroyer flotillas. Each squadron had a leader (a Porter-class destroyer) and two four-destroyer divisions. Except for one division of flush-deck destroyers assigned to the West Coast (not shown), all of these were new construction, built after 1934.

Destroyers were assigned to task forces at sea, either the main battle line or carrier and cruiser task forces. Typically, they were assigned by squadron, although occasionally only a division would be sent. Destroyers were intended to launch torpedo attacks against enemy surface ships and screen cruisers, carriers and battleships from submarines and torpedo-carrying surface warships.

Three aircraft carriers and their air groups (60 to 90 aircraft) were typically accompanied by a cruiser division and a destroyer flotilla. These were assigned ad hoc as available.

The only surface warships in Scouting Force were the heavy cruisers. Too weak to trade broadsides with battleships, with main guns that fired too slowly to stop torpedo attacks, they were not used in the battle line. Instead, they scouted, performed missions which required fast, powerful ships, or showed the flag at foreign ports. They also protected carriers from attack, being fast enough to keep up with them and strong enough to fight anything else that could keep up. The Pacific Fleet had three four-ship cruiser divisions in Scouting Force.

Scouting Force also had five submarine divisions, split between two flotillas. Each division was supposed to have six submarines, although two had only three. Only four divisions had fleet submarines, one made up of older, smaller S-boats, confined to operating off the North American West Coast. The rest were primarily intended as scouts, to seek out and attack enemy warships (see p.25).

Aircraft, Scouting Force was the final Scouting Force organization. It comprised three patrol wings with three to four patrol squadrons (VPs) and one independent VP. These were Patrol Wing 1 (VP11, VP12, VP14), Patrol Wing 2 (VP22, VP23, VP24), Patrol Wing 4 (VP41, VP42, VP43, VP14), and the independent VP13. Each patrol wing had four to six seaplane tenders (AV, AVP, AVD) supporting them.

The fleet as shown here represents a perfect organization. In reality, one-eighth to one-quarter of the ships would be unavailable, in dry dock for routine maintenance or the numerous upgrades to warships in 1941. In wartime, battle damage and losses would further affect the organization.

This organization had several flaws revealed only in combat. Examples include gross underestimation of Japanese torpedo capabilities and flawed carrier doctrine.

in. Some changes could mitigate these threats, such as improved damage control, better compartmentalization and anti-torpedo blisters, but this addressed the problems at the margins. The best defense against both U-boats and aircraft was speed, which the US battleships conspicuously lacked.

Nor could these issues be addressed by new construction. The battleship-building race spurred by the end of World War I had strained the finances of all major naval powers and was driving Japan to bankruptcy. This led to a naval arms limitation conference resulting in the Washington Treaty, which killed most current construction and put a ten-year "holiday" on new dreadnought construction. The pause was extended another six years at future conferences.

The battleships on hand in 1923 had to soldier on well past their original intended lifespan of 20 years. Throughout the 1920s and 1930s, the US Navy modernized and rebuilt its battleship fleet, including those in the Pacific Fleet. Some changes corrected design flaws or replaced obsolete equipment. Torpedo tubes were removed, as were the casemate 5in./51cal guns located below the upper deck. Main battery range made torpedoes useless. Casemate guns below the upper deck were too close to the waterline, posing a flooding hazard. Their numbers were reduced and they were placed on the upper deck, a battleship's weather deck. The main guns of all Pacific Fleet battleships were replaced in the 1930s with upgraded versions that fired larger shells at greater ranges.

Other changes addressed the increasing influence of aircraft. Provisions for aircraft were added, with catapults and cranes to permit the battleships to operate seaplanes, which would be used for reconnaissance and gunnery spotting. Throughout the 1920s and 1930s, antiaircraft batteries were constantly upgraded, and, as built, battleships were outfitted with a few 3in./50cal antiaircraft guns. During refits, these were replaced by 5in./25cal antiaircraft guns, and the number of antiaircraft guns increased.

By 1941, the Pacific Fleet's battleships achieved remarkable uniformity. All carried 12 casemate-mounted 5in./51cal on their upper deck, and eight to 12 5in./25cal on the superstructure as an antiaircraft battery. These were supplemented with eight .50cal machine guns. The US Navy planned to add quad 1.1in. machine guns to upgrade light antiaircraft capabilities. In addition, all had two catapults (one on the superfiring "X" turret and one on the quarterdeck), and three floatplanes.

Aircraft Carriers

The aircraft carrier was the newest category of warship present in the US Pacific Fleet in 1941. It began its existence with four aircraft carriers. Present throughout the US Pacific Fleet's first year of existence were the two Lexington-class aircraft carriers, *Lexington* and *Saratoga*. Two Yorktown-class aircraft carriers, *Yorktown* and *Enterprise,* were also in the Pacific Fleet in February 1941. *Yorktown* was withdrawn to the Atlantic in May 1941.

Aircraft carriers appeared immediately prior to World War I. Initially, the aircraft carried were seaplanes, although by 1918 ships capable of landing as well as launching aircraft existed. After World War I, all of those ships belonged to the Royal Navy. No one else built them during World War I, including the United States. Before World War I, the US Navy's General Board was hostile

Lexington was originally intended as a battlecruiser. Instead completed as an aircraft carrier. It and its sister *Saratoga* were the world's largest aircraft carriers until *Shinano* in 1944. They were the longest until *Midway* arrived in 1945. (USNHHC)

to the idea of aircraft operating off ships, fearing that naval ships would end up only as fuel depots for aircraft.

By 1919, the US Navy had altered its views. The Royal Navy had four aircraft carriers (although two were incomplete, construction being paused at war's end) and Japan was laying the keel for its first aircraft carrier, *Hosho*. The US Navy decided to investigate these new contraptions, beginning conversion of the collier *Jupiter* to a carrier in 1920. In 1922, it was commissioned as CV-1, USS *Langley*. It was not completely satisfactory, slow and lacking a hangar deck, but it proved a useful testbed for US Navy carrier operations and development of doctrine.

As with much of the 1941 US Pacific Fleet, the Washington Treaty changed US Navy carrier aviation. It permitted conversion of excess dreadnoughts to aircraft carriers. Several nations took advantage of that clause. Britain converted its "large light cruisers" *Courageous* and *Glorious* (to join half-sister *Furious* as a division of three 30-knot carriers). France transformed the moldering, half-built battleship *Béarn* into a carrier. Japan salvaged the unfinished battle cruisers *Amagi* and *Akagi* for transformation. (They substituted the half-built battleship *Kaga* for *Amagi* after an earthquake destroyed the latter.)

The United States was building six battlecruisers which had to be scrapped under provisions of the treaty. They chose two, *Lexington* and *Saratoga,* for conversion to aircraft carriers. The result was impressive. The hulls displaced 38,000 tons, and had a waterline length of 850ft with a 104ft 7in. beam. They retained the 7in. belt armor and the 180,000shp turbines intended for the battle cruisers. The hull remained largely unchanged to the upper deck. A massive hangar was added above the hull, 450ft long, 70ft wide and 21ft deep. The hangar was topped by a flight deck 880ft long and 106ft wide. There was one catapult to launch aircraft on the flight deck, and two elevators to move aircraft from the hangar deck to the flight deck. The superstructure was amidships, on the starboard side. It contained a long rectangular funnel with the bridge structure ahead of it.

The finished vessels were fast and could reach 33.25 knots using turbo-electric drive. They had an unrefueled range of 10,000nm at 15 knots. They were heavily armed, and, designed to operate an 80-aircraft air group in the 1920s when they were first commissioned. They could have carried many more. Even with the larger aircraft of World War II, each could easily accommodate 80 aircraft. When commissioned, they also carried 12 5in./25cal antiaircraft guns in single mounts and eight 8in./55cal guns in four twin mounts, ahead of the superstructure and aft of the funnel.

Giving an aircraft carrier a heavy cruiser's main battery seems odd to modern eyes, but it should be viewed from a contemporary standpoint. In the mid-1920s, when the conversion was planned, aircraft carrier doctrine was being developed. Aircraft were slow and fragile, and could not operate at night or in bad weather. The guns were seen as

Saratoga prepared to launch aircraft in fall 1941. F4F Wildcats are at the front, with SBD Dauntlesses behind them and TBD Devastators at the back. Size allowed Lexington-class ships to carry many aircraft. On December 7, 1941, *Saratoga* had an air group of 88 airplanes. (USNHHC)

an opportunity to protect the carriers at night and in stormy seas. Since no navy had ever operated a large carrier when the Lexingtons were built, this seemed reasonable. By 1941, plans were in hand to replace the 8in. turrets with twin 5in./38cal turrets on the same barbettes.

The conversion gave the US Navy the world's largest and fastest aircraft carriers. They would not be exceeded in displacement until *Shinano*, originally intended as a Yamato-class battleship, was launched in October 1944. Even then, the *Saratoga*, surviving ship of its class, was longer. Only after the Midway class arrived in 1945, did the US Navy have a bigger aircraft carrier.

While imperfect as carrier designs, they gave the US Navy a marvelous laboratory to test naval aviation. An individual Lexington could carry an air group of a size that required two or even three carriers with other navies. The US Navy took advantage of this, using the carriers for wide-ranging naval exercises testing the limits of naval aviation. This included using them to conduct mass air attacks against Hawaii and the Panama Canal. As aircraft grew in capability, these two aircraft carriers grew in power.

They made another contribution to carrier aviation. The US Navy planned to name battlecruisers after famous naval warships and significant military victories, and the names were retained after conversion. Thereafter, until *Franklin D. Roosevelt* was launched in April 1945, all subsequent fleet and light carriers retained that custom.

The Pacific Fleet also had two Yorktown-class aircraft carriers. This was the second attempt at a "keel-up" aircraft carrier design by the US Navy. It was a successful design, much more than the preceding (and much smaller) *Ranger*. The design was hostage to naval limitations treaties, which limited displacement to 20,000 tons. As the *Nevada* did for US battleships, the *Yorktown* proved the model for future US Navy carriers.

They were smaller than the Lexingtons, and *Yorktown* and *Enterprise* displaced 19,872 tons when completed. They were 770ft long at the waterline, with a beam of 83.25ft, and the flight deck was 809.5ft by 86ft. At 120,000shp, the machinery had two-thirds the power of *Lexington's* plant, but Yorktowns could reach 32.5 knots, within a knot of *Lexington's* top speed. They had a range of 12,000nm at 15 knots.

They lacked the armor and 8in. battery of their big sisters, carrying eight 5in./38cal guns in single mounts. In 1941, they had four quad 1.1in. guns and

Enterprise was the newest carrier in the Pacific Fleet. Along with sister *Yorktown*, it was the US Navy's first completely successful keel-up carrier design. Here, it is operating in the Pacific in June 1941. It became the most renowned carrier of World War II. (USNHHC)

24 .50cal machine guns. To save weight, the armor belt was 4in. maximum, covering only machinery spaces, and geared turbines drove the four propellers. A 1in. armor deck sat above the machinery. To compensate for the reduced armor, there was more extensive subdivision of the lower hull, improving damage control.

As with the Lexingtons, the hangar was placed on the upper deck and topped by the flight deck. Unlike the Lexingtons, the gap between the upper deck and flight deck was not completely plated over. This permitted better ventilation and easier replenishment under way. The openings could be closed by rolling shutters, when necessary. The island was again on the starboard side, with the funnels aft of the bridge structure. They had three elevators and three catapults, although one was on the hangar deck and rarely used. Officially, they could carry 90 aircraft, although that became crowded; normally no more than 80 were carried.

The carriers entered service in 1937 and 1938 respectively. A sixth (and final) aircraft carrier built within naval treaty constraints, *Wasp*, was commissioned

CARRIER DOCTRINE IN 1941

By May 1941, the Pacific Fleet had three aircraft carriers. Due to the difference in speed of the carriers and the battleships, the carriers operated in task forces independently of the battleships. Since the carriers were scarce and valuable, they typically operated individually, one carrier to a task force. The belief was that this avoided putting too many eggs in one basket, so if a carrier task force was caught, only one carrier was at risk. It would take actual war experience before the force multiplier effect of massed carriers was understood.

This diagram shows how a carrier group would be used. The top part shows the task force seeking an enemy fleet, with the blue disc representing the task force. A blow-up shows how the ships were arranged, with the carrier in the middle surrounded by three cruisers from the heavy cruiser division guarding it. (The fourth was undergoing refit and unavailable.) A ring of nine destroyers circles the larger ship, providing antiaircraft and antisubmarine protection. There are also four F4Fs aloft providing combat air patrol.

Each carrier had two SBD scout bomber squadrons, each comprising 12 to 22 SBDs. One was a scout squadron, sent out to search for the enemy and flying wedge-shaped searches along an arc where enemy ships could be operating. This diagram shows operations if the enemy location is unknown and there is no other source of airborne reconnaissance. Thirteen of the 18 SBDs in the scout squadron are flying search patterns looking for enemy ships (the red disc). (The rest are refueling, undergoing maintenance or unavailable.)

Once the enemy is located, an air strike is launched as shown in the bottom part. A deckload strike (a full flight deck of aircraft) is sent: 15 TBD Devastator torpedo bombers, 18 SBDs (the bombing squadron) and 16 F4Fs Wildcat as escort. The slow Devastators launch first, followed by the Dauntlesses, with the fighters, the fastest aircraft, launching last. This allows the three groups of aircraft to arrive over the target at the same time, to launch a coordinated strike. The TBDs fly 1,000–2,000ft above the ocean, for a torpedo attack. The SBDs climb until they reach 20,000–23,000ft, dive-bombing altitude. The fighters split the difference, flying 5,000–12,000ft so they can cover either the TBDs or SBDs as required.

To assist in recovery of the attacking aircraft post strike, the carrier moves closer to the enemy formation, moving from location 1 to location 2 by the time the aircraft are returning. The aircraft are given a rendezvous point pre-mission. If required, the carrier might broadcast a homing beacon to help the returning aircraft.

This diagram shows how an attack is *supposed* to occur. Reality had a way of intruding, as happened at Midway in June 1942, where the TBDs, SBDs and F4Fs lost sight of each other and attacked piecemeal, allowing enemy fighters to slaughter the Devastators.

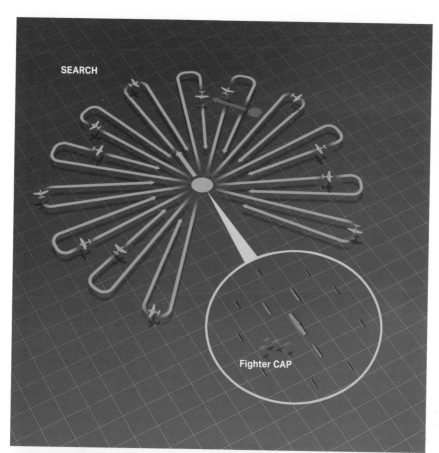

SEARCH

Fighter CAP

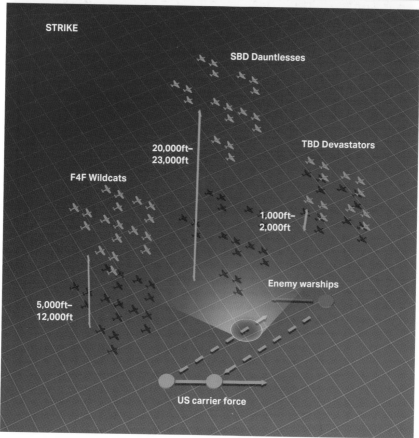

STRIKE

SBD Dauntlesses

TBD Devastators

20,000ft–23,000ft

F4F Wildcats

1,000ft–2,000ft

Enemy warships

5,000ft–12,000ft

US carrier force

in 1940. To fit within tonnage limitations, it displaced only 14,700 tons, but future carriers discarded treaty tonnage and design limitations. *Hornet*, built after the treaty lapsed, used the existing Yorktown design to save time. It was commissioned in October 1941.

Cruisers

Three types of cruisers belonged to the Pacific Fleet in 1941: the pre-treaty scout cruisers of the Omaha class, cruisers carrying an 8in. battery designed to the standards of the 1922 Washington Treaty, and cruisers with a 6in. main battery built to the standards of the 1930 London Treaty. By 1941, all cruisers with 6in. main batteries were classified light cruisers while all cruisers with 8in. batteries were classified heavy cruisers.

In reality, US Navy cruisers of World War II shared more with unarmored scout and lightly armored protected cruisers of World War I than with that period's heavily armored (and gunned) armored cruisers. Regardless of size, all were lightly armored and fast. The first heavy cruisers built for the US Navy were originally rated light cruisers for their armor and speed. They were upgraded to heavy cruisers, a new category (as opposed to the traditional "armored cruiser" their "CA" hull identifier implied) following ratification of the London Treaty in 1930.

This treaty-motivated upgrade was why the US Navy numbered heavy (CA) and light (CL) in a combined sequence rather than using independent number sequences for the two classes (as they did with aircraft carriers – CVs, or Cruiser, aViation – and the future Alaska-class "large" cruisers – which became "CBs"). The treaty cruisers, light and heavy, were built to the maximum size permitted by naval limitations treaties, 10,000 tons.

The oldest cruisers in the Pacific Fleet were the Omaha-class light cruisers. In December 1941, the Pacific Fleet had half the ten Omaha-class cruisers in commission. Three, *Trenton*, *Richmond* and *Concord*, belonged to Cruiser Division 3 with the Battle Force. Two others, *Raleigh* and *Detroit*, were flagships for destroyer flotillas. They were designed as and started their careers as scout cruisers, fast, lightly armored and armed cruisers, intended to lead destroyers and scout the enemy's position. It was a vital role played exclusively by ships before and during World War I, when these ships were designed. They were reclassified as light cruisers in the 1920s.

They were multi-purpose warships. In addition to scouting, they were intended to protect the battle line from enemy destroyer attacks, protect convoys from surface raiders, serve as destroyer flotilla leaders, and act as minelayers. The mine racks could carry depth charges and they carried hydrophones, allowing them

Northampton was the lead ship of the US Navy's second batch of treaty cruisers. Photographed entering Brisbane during a show-the-flag cruise, it has a fake bow wave painted on as camouflage. Its CXAM radar antenna is on the foremast. *Northampton* was one of the first Navy warships to get radar. (USNHHC)

to fill antisubmarine roles. They were 555ft 6in. long, with a 55ft 4in. beam and a 20ft draft. They displaced 7,050 tons standard and 9,508 tons fully loaded. With four shafts and 90,000shp steam turbine engines, their maximum speed was 35 knots when new.

As built, they carried 12 6in./53cal main guns (four in two twin turrets with eight casemate-mounted single guns), two 3in./50cal antiaircraft guns, ten 21in. torpedo tubes and 224 mines. By World War II, this changed. The ships had proven wet and top-heavy. Also, aircraft, insignificant when they were designed, grew in importance during the 1920s and 1930s.

To reduce topside weight, the minelaying racks, the lower set of casemate 6in. guns and two twin-torpedo tubes were removed, leaving the ships with six torpedo tubes and a main battery of ten 6in. guns. The secondary antiaircraft battery was increased to eight 3in. guns with two or three quad 1.1in. guns added. Two catapults for floatplanes were added. By 1941, these ships were obsolescent and their scouting duties had been transferred to aircraft. Cruisers were no longer expected to be used for torpedo attacks. Too weak to be considered major combatants, they were relegated to secondary duties.

The 8in. or heavy cruisers were the next-oldest cruisers in the Pacific Fleet. By December 1941, the fleet had 12 of the 17 heavy cruisers in commission in the US Navy. These included the two Pensacola-class, four of the six Northampton-class, the two Portland-class, and four of the six New Orleans-class cruisers. The Pensacola-class cruisers had a main battery of ten 8in./55cal guns. All others were armed with nine 8in./55cal guns. By 1941, all carried eight 5in./25cal antiaircraft guns, along with a mix of .50cal machine guns and quad 1.1in. antiaircraft guns.

All were designed to exactly fit the limits of the Washington Treaty. They carried the largest guns permitted (8in.) and displaced as close to the treaty limit of 10,000 tons as possible. Design uncertainties led the Pensacolas and Northamptons to a standard displacement of 9,100 and 9,050 tons respectively. This was corrected by the New Orleans class, which was fast, with a top speed of at least 32.5 knots, requiring large engines and boilers. (All used steam turbines.)

Little was left over for armor, leading to initial classification as light cruisers. All were equipped with armor belts previously associated with light and protected cruisers, rather than armored cruisers traditionally carrying 8in. main batteries. The early treaty cruisers had maximum belt armor of 2.5in. to 3.5in. (The later New Orleans class used much of the 1,000-ton allowance to increase armor thickness.) They were often categorized as "tinclad" cruisers and described as "eggshells armed with hammers."

They represented a leap in cruiser size. Before and during World War I, light cruisers with few exceptions (such as the Royal Navy's Hawkins class and the Omahas) typically displaced between 4,000 and 6,000 tons. This remained a good size (especially the upper range, 6,000 tons) for the Royal Navy, then still the world's largest. While the Royal Navy joined the 10,000-ton, 8in. cruiser race, its needs were better met by large numbers of smaller cruisers.

Light cruiser *Honolulu* (CL-48) was built after the 1930 London Treaty. Its 6in. main battery was a concession to Britain, which wanted to stop the heavy cruiser race. Its size, 10,000 tons with 15 main guns, frustrated British desire to reduce cruiser sizes. (USNHHC)

This led to the 1930 London Treaty, which allowed completion of the 8in. cruisers ordered under the Washington Treaty, but limited most future cruiser construction to a main battery of 6in. guns. Royal Navy planners expected this would see a return to smaller cruiser sizes, and the Royal Navy laid down 12 such vessels between 1930 and 1936.

Neither Japan nor the United States followed that path. Both used their light cruisers' tonnage allocated by the 1930 London Treaty to build the biggest permissible vessels with the greatest possible firepower. For the US, this resulted in the Brooklyn class, of which nine were built, including two in the slightly modified St Louis subclass. These were big: 9,767 to 9,824 tons standard displacement, an overall length of 608ft 4in., and a top speed of 32.5 knots.

Each carried a main battery of 15 6in./47cal guns mounted in five triple turrets, and each gun could pump out up to 13 shells a minute. (The official rate of fire was ten rounds a minute.) Fired continuously, they could empty their magazines in under a dozen minutes. Most also carried eight 5in./25cal antiaircraft guns. The two St Louis-class ships replaced these with the superior 5in./38cal gun. To support scouting duties, they carried four floatplanes launched from two quarterdeck-mounted catapults.

The firehose of shells the Brooklyns produced was intended to help these cruisers protect the battle line from destroyer torpedo attack. Five of these ships were assigned to the Pacific Fleet's Battle Force, in Cruiser Squadron 9 directly supporting the battle line.

The Brooklyn class carried the same armor protection as the New Orleans-class heavy cruisers, and by then, the main difference between US heavy and light cruisers was their main battery guns. Except for the Atlanta class, all subsequent World War II-era US Navy cruisers were developments of the Brooklyns, both the light cruiser Cleveland class and the heavy cruiser Wichita and Baltimore classes.

All treaty cruisers were designed for Pacific operations, could steam at least 10,000nm at 15 knots, and were capable of underway refueling. While some of the older treaty cruisers were built with torpedo tubes, all were removed during the 1930s: Unique among the world's cruisers, their guns were their only weapons. All could serve as independent raiders, support the battle line, or provide antiaircraft support.

Destroyers

The Pacific Fleet had 50 destroyers in December 1941. When created, it had more, but a destroyer squadron was transferred to the Atlantic in April 1941. It could also call upon the nine destroyers assigned to Naval Districts within the US Pacific Fleet's boundaries, although these were intended for local defense, and not fleet operations.

Of the 50 destroyers, four were from flush-deck Wickes and Clemson classes mass-produced between 1916 and 1923. (As were eight of the nine Naval District destroyers; the ninth belonged to an even older class.) Flush-deck destroyers were designed before aircraft and submarines posed a real threat, and had inadequate antiaircraft and antisubmarine capabilities. They had a main battery of 4in. guns and were older and slower than later construction.

By 1941, these ships were obsolescent, useful only for littoral and harbor defense, antisubmarine convoy escort and training. Assignment of these ships reflected that. Four Pacific Fleet flush-deck destroyers were training ships. The fifth served as flagship for a submarine squadron, a harbor assignment.

The remaining destroyers belonged to classes built between 1933 and 1939: the Farragut, Porter, Mahan, Gridley, Bagley and Benham classes. They had been built in that order, although the Porters were constructed almost concurrently with the Farragut and Mahan classes. All conformed to the 1930 London Treaty.

The Farragut, Mahan and Gridley classes were the most heavily influenced by the 1930 London Treaty. These ships all had a standard displacement at or under 1,500 tons. Bagleys and Benhams were larger, between 1,624 and 1,656 tons standard displacement. The Porter class, intended as destroyer leaders, was larger, 1,850 standard tons, and Porters served as destroyer squadron flagships.

All were multi-purpose vessels, capable of fighting submarines, aircraft and surface ships. All had sonar gear, and all except the Farraguts were built with two aft depth charge racks (later added to the Farraguts). All had a main battery of 5in./38cal dual-purpose guns, effective against aircraft or surface targets, and carried 21in. torpedo tubes. While the main battery provided excellent heavy antiaircraft capabilities, all had inadequate light antiaircraft armament: two to four single 0.50cal machine guns.

The mix of torpedo tubes and main guns carried varied by class. The Farragut and Porter classes carried eight torpedo tubes in two centerline quad mounts. The Mahans had 12 torpedo tubes in quad mounts with one mounted centerline and one each on the port and starboard sides. The Gridley, Bagley and Benham

Farragut was the lead ship of the first destroyers the US Navy built since the World War I-era flush-deck destroyers. They were intended to operate with the battle line. Their antisubmarine and antiaircraft capabilities were weak. (USNHHC)

classes had four quad mounts, two on each side. The Farragut and Mahan classes had five 5in./38cal guns in single mounts, while the Gridley, Bagley and Benham classes carried four. The Porters had eight 5in./38s in four twin turrets.

All were fast, delivering a top speed of 37 knots or higher at trials. The Farraguts had engines producing 42,000shp; the rest had powerplants generating 47,000 to 50,000shp. By contrast, the Clemson class, preceding the Farraguts, had steam plants generating only 27,600shp. Enhanced horsepower was achieved by powerplants using higher temperatures and higher pressures than the flush-deck destroyers.

One peculiarity about these destroyers was their weak antisubmarine capability and relatively low ammunition storage. The Farraguts were built without depth-charge racks, and all lacked side-mounted K-gun depth-charge launchers, despite space to accommodate them. Similarly, the as-built light antiaircraft batteries were inadequate, but this was done to maximize destroyer numbers while remaining within treaty limits. If war broke out, the Navy planned to add these during refits. Magazines were sized to accommodate more ammunition than carried during peacetime.

The effort to cram as much fighting capability into the smallest possible displacement meant these treaty designs, especially the Farragut, Porter and Mahan classes, were built top-heavy. Adding more weight topside made this worse. However, except for the Farraguts, which installed depth-charge racks after the naval treaties expired, in 1941 none of the destroyers had wartime refits, which exacerbated stability problems.

Another compromise to save weight for treaty purposes was the placement of engine rooms and boiler rooms. All these designs had two engine rooms and two boiler rooms in separate watertight compartments. A destroyer could operate with one of each. Both engine rooms were adjacent to each other as were both boiler rooms.

A torpedo hit that opened two machinery compartments had a two-thirds chance of knocking out both boiler rooms or both engine rooms, leaving the vessel dead in the water. Worse, until the Mahan class, destroyers were not fitted with emergency diesel generators to provide electrical power for pumps and other equipment. If the engines went out, power was available only until the batteries were exhausted.

Size also limited their range. Unrefueled, they could only steam 5,300 to 7,000nm, and that at 12 knots. At combat speeds, it could be one-third of that. Running with low fuel tanks exacerbated stability problems. Fuel bunkers were in the lowest part of the hull and, unless ballasted with seawater, empty tanks raised the tipping point dangerously. Once the bunker was filled with seawater, it could not store fuel until cleaned thoroughly to remove salt. Refueling at sea eased this range limitation.

Eight Farragut-class destroyers of Destroyer Division 2 practice a daytime torpedo run at enemy warships. Steaming in line abreast, they cut through a smokescreen laid by PBY Patrol Bombers to shield them from enemy view. They were never employed this way during the Pacific War. (USNHHC)

Treaty destroyers carried more torpedo tubes than most destroyers of most of the world's navies, including the Japanese. (Japanese torpedoes were far more powerful than US torpedoes, but in 1941, no one outside Japan realized that.) They also carried reloads for the torpedo tubes. One reason for the heavy torpedo batteries was to compensate for the lack of torpedoes on US Navy cruisers.

The heavy torpedo batteries also fitted US Navy doctrine of the period, which envisioned the Pacific Fleet's destroyers launching mass torpedo attacks against the Japanese battle line. The classes with 16 torpedo tubes had two sets mounted on each side, and these ships were thought capable of launching all 16 in one salvo using "curved ahead attacks." The destroyers discharged all tubes, and used gyro settings in the torpedo to steer them to a single target.

While mass torpedo attacks against Japanese battle lines proved illusory, the 5in. main batteries gave these destroyers real stopping power against smaller surface warships as they were intended to break up a Japanese torpedo attack against the US battle line. It also meant they had the best antiaircraft capability of any other nation's contemporary destroyers. They proved the right designs for the challenges of the Pacific War.

Submarines

The 1941 Pacific Fleet had 24 submarines. Six were S-boats, operating off the North American coast. The other 18 were stationed at Pearl Harbor. Three were special submarines, the minelayer *Argonaut*, and two large cruiser submarines, *Nautilus* and *Narwhal*. The remaining ones were fleet submarines of the Dolphin, Catchalot, Perch, Tambor and Gar classes.

All submarines belonged to Scouting Force. This reflected their intended purpose. Fleet submarines were expected to serve as scouts for the Battle Force. They were to provide a screen operating ahead of the Battle Force to detect an approaching Japanese force. If possible, after reporting contact, they were to pick off a battleship or cruiser.

This requirement drove the design of the fleet boats (US submariners always referred to submarines as boats). They had to keep up with the fleet. The oldest of these fleet boats, the Dolphin, Catchalot and Perch classes, could make 17 or 18 knots on the surface, and up to 8 knots submerged. The Tambor and Gar classes could make 20.4 knots surfaced, fast enough to keep up with the battleships.

They were also long range. The Catchalots, Tambors and Gars had a range of 11,000nm at 10 knots surfaced. The three Perch-class submarines, *Plunger*, *Pollack* and *Pompano*, could make only 6,000nm, and were more limited. The elderly *Dolphin* (launched in 1932, and the true prototype "fleet boat") had a range of only 4,900nm using dedicated fuel tanks, but could carry fuel in its ballast tanks. That gave it a range of 18,800nm.

They were also large. While typical Royal Navy and Kriegsmarine submarines were 500 to 1,100 tons, the smallest fleet submarine in the US Pacific Fleet was 1,100 tons. Most displaced between 1,300 and 1,450 tons surfaced, and

Dolphin displaced 1,718 tons. They were 260 to 319ft long. Only Japan had submarines of comparable or larger sizes.

The oldest three classes had six 21in. torpedo tubes (four forward and two a stern) and carried 16 or 18 torpedoes. The Tambor and Gar classes had ten torpedo tubes (six forward and four aft) and 16 21in. torpedoes. All but *Dolphin* were armed with one 3in. deck gun, and *Dolphin* had a 4in. deck gun. (The London Treaty limited deck guns to a maximum 5in. bore.)

A major reason for the large number of torpedo tubes was they were intended to operate against battleships, aircraft carriers and large cruisers. A single hit would likely sink a merchantman or many small warships, but big ships took multiple hits. With a spread of four, or better still, six torpedoes, the odds of getting hits increased, and multiple hits were more likely.

FLEET SUBMARINE DOCTRINE IN 1941

While the US Navy's World War II submarine service was renowned for its destruction of Japan's merchant marine, it was not built for that purpose. Before the war, it was barred by US Navy doctrine and international law from conducting unlimited submarine warfare. Rather, submarines were built to support the surface fleet. They were large, fast, long-ranged and heavily armed, with up to ten torpedo tubes. They could keep up with the battle line (although not carrier and cruiser formations) if necessary.

Under normal circumstances, the submarines were used for long-range scouting, as shown here. It assumes a (then) hypothetical war with Japan and an expected Japanese invasion of Wake. (Prewar Pacific Fleet plans used Wake as bait, to lure the Japanese main battle fleet there.)

In this example, the submarines are being used as advance scouts beyond the range of long-range aerial reconnaissance. Although the Pacific Fleet had 15 fleet submarines, one-third would be unavailable, traveling or under maintenance. The ten available submarines would be spread along two lines (1) covering the most likely approaches to Wake, from Saipan in the Marianas or Truk in the Carolines. Although the distance from Japan to Saipan was shorter, Truk would have been seen as the more likely of the two as the US assumed Japan had a fortified naval base there. (In reality, it was an almost unimproved anchorage.) The lines are set well beyond effective maritime air search range to provide advance warning of any enemy movement towards Wake.

A Japanese fleet sorties from Truk (2). One submarine on the Truk picket line detects it (3) as it moves to Wake from Truk. The submarine's commander reports the contact (including time, location, and direction of the enemy force). After that, the commander is free to attempt an attack on the ships. Other subs on the Truk picket line try to close on the enemy using the contact report relayed to them (4).

The submarines on the Saipan line use the contact report to set up a submarine ambush close to Wake (5). Two conditions are required for this to work: the submarines have to travel surfaced at flank speed to reach the ambush point, and the invasion force has to be slowed enough by the transports to allow the submarines to reach the ambush point ahead of the Japanese. Meanwhile, alerted by the submarine's warning, a Battle Force relief force from Pearl Harbor nears Wake.

This doctrine assumes no direct knowledge of the enemy fleet, that the submarines are searching blind with no outside information of the enemy fleet's location. However, as 1941 progressed, signal intelligence, a combination of codebreaking and radio direction-finding, removed the need to use submarines for this type of long-range reconnaissance. Instead of using submarines to locate the enemy, they were directed to the enemy through signal intelligence.

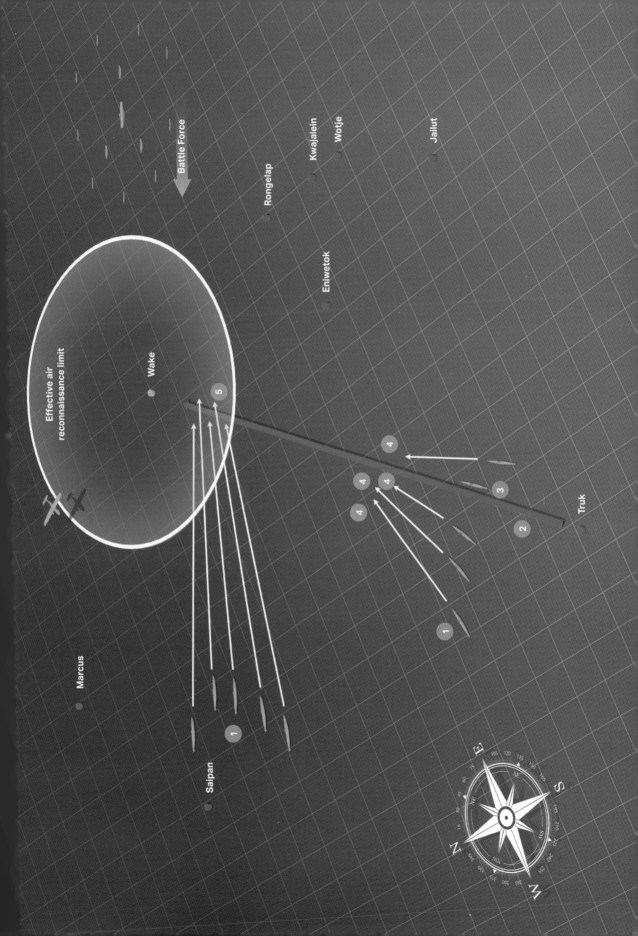

Grayling was one of three Gar-class submarines in the 1941 Pacific Fleet. A subclass of the Tambor class, *Grayling* had ten torpedo tubes. Fast and long-ranged, fleet submarines were intended to operate with the fleet against warships. (USNHHC)

One weakness was they could not dive very deep. The test depth of all but the Tambor and Gar classes was 250ft, while Tambors and Gars had a test depth of 300ft. By contrast, German U-boats had a test depth of 750ft. On the other hand, Japanese submarines could only dive 150ft, and Japanese antisubmarine warfare doctrine assumed this was the maximum depth US submarines could reach.

Argonaut, and two large cruiser submarines, *Nautilus* and *Narwhal,* were built in the late 1920s, the only US Pacific Fleet large submarines built prior to the First London Treaty. Unconstrained by the treaty, all three displaced over 2,700 tons surfaced, carried two 6in. deck guns and had a test depth of 300ft. Built as cruising submarines, optimized for raiding against sea lanes, this was dropped after ratification of the First London Treaty. Thereafter, they were used as fleet submarines, albeit larger and more awkward than the newer fleet boats.

Argonaut, built as a minelayer, had an overall length of 381ft, and carried four 21in. bow torpedo tubes and two 40in. minelaying tubes aft. In 1941, it carried 16 torpedoes and 60 mines. It had a maximum surface speed of 15 knots and an 8,000nm range at 10 knots surfaced, or 18,000nm if it carried fuel in its ballast tanks. *Narwhal* and *Nautilus* were 371ft long overall, carried six 21in. torpedo tubes (four forward, two aft) with 24 torpedoes (including six in deck stowage). They had a top surface speed of 17.4 knots with a 9,380nm range at 10 knots (25,000nm using fuel in the ballast tanks).

Submarines operated independently. More than any other naval vessel, they reflected their commanding officer. An aggressive, competent captain made for an effective submarine, particularly when pressing a lone attack against an enemy fleet, while a cautious, reluctant captain yielded an ineffective, poorly performing boat.

Auxiliaries

Perhaps the most important ships in the 1941 US Pacific Fleet were the auxiliary warships and fleet auxiliaries assigned to it. Often overlooked, they proved critical during the Pacific War. Their importance was understood by the US Navy before the war. The United States had no real bases west of Pearl Harbor except in the Philippines (expected to be under siege shortly after any war with Japan began). War plans called for the Pacific Fleet to cross the Central Pacific, relieve the Philippines and then besiege Japan, thousands of miles from Hawaii.

This required the Pacific Fleet to bring the beans, bullets and black oil needed by the fleet with them. They needed to set up forward bases with aviation, maintenance and repair facilities as they advanced. They needed to capture islands to house those bases, which meant they must clear minefields and dredge harbors. That would be handled by the fleet train, which had four broad categories: mine warfare vessels, replenishment vessels, support vessels and base vessels.

The Pacific Fleet had 13 transports, ships intended to move troops across the Pacific. Large ships, the smallest displaced 8,000 tons, the largest 21,000 tons. Each carried 1,000 to 2,000 troops. Eight dated to World War I; five were new construction. Older transports had top speeds of 12 to 14 knots, while new construction transports, built between 1938 and 1941, could steam at up to 18 knots. In 1941, the US Pacific Fleet's Amphibious Force consisted of two divisions, one Army infantry division and the 2nd Marine Division. Transports and troops were to support the US Pacific Fleet's Central Pacific drive, invading and occupying islands.

The Pacific Fleet had 30 mine warfare vessels: 21 minesweepers and nine minelayers. Thirteen minesweepers belonged to the fleet's Battle Force, eight to its Base Force. All nine minelayers were in the Battle Force. The ratio reveals the relative importance of those activities. Minesweeping was needed offensively (to clear approaches to landing beaches) and defensively (maintaining swept channels). Minelayers were primarily defensive. They were to protect ports and anchorages taken during an advance.

Most Pacific Fleet mine warfare vessels, eight minelayers and 13 minesweepers, were converted from Clemson- and Wickes-class destroyers. Minelaying conversions replaced the torpedo tubes with mine racks capable of carrying 80 mines, rebuilt the stern and relocated depth-charge racks. The minesweeper conversion removed one boiler and the torpedo tubes and added minesweeping gear. Since they retained their sonar and carried depth charges, they could be used as convoy escorts.

The Pacific Fleet also had the minelayer *Oglala*, a 3,800-ton vessel converted to a minelayer during World War I and retained. It served as squadron flagship for Pacific Fleet Mine Squadron 1. Service Squadron 6, with eight Lapwing-class minesweepers, filled out the Pacific Fleet's mine warfare collection. These were 840-ton vessels built in World War I. Although these vessels were minesweepers, other Lapwings served as oceangoing tugs, seaplane tenders, salvage ships and submarine rescue vessels.

Replenishment vessels were those providing provisions, supplies, munitions and fuel to the fleet. These included general stores issue ships, provisions stores ships, ammunition ships and fleet oilers. These could be supplemented by Base

In February 1941, *Platte* was one of 12 fleet oilers in the US Pacific Fleet. A new Cimarron-class oiler, it was commissioned in 1939. These oilers carried 16,500DWT of fuel oil, and had a top speed of 18.3 knots. (USNHHC)

Force transports and cargo ships. In December 1941, the Pacific Fleet had two general stores issue ships, four provisions stores ships, two ammunition ships, 11 fleet oilers and four cargo ships.

The fleet oilers were the most important replenishment ships. They kept the fleet fueled and could refuel ships at sea, while under way. One was built before World War I, and six between 1915 and 1922. Four were new construction, Cimarron-class oilers commissioned in 1939 and 1940.

All were big ships. The seven older oilers were between 447ft and 475ft long. They displaced 14,700 to 17,800 tons fully loaded. The smallest could supply ships with up to 7,843 deadweight tons (DWT) of fuel oil and the largest held 11,100DWT. Their biggest drawback was their slow speed. Their top speed ranged from 11.2 to 14.3 knots. The Cimarron-class oilers were bigger and faster. They were 553ft long, displaced 25,425 tons loaded (of which 16,500DWT was fuel oil cargo), and could make 18.3 knots.

Their ability to refuel ships at sea, under way, gave the Pacific Fleet its mobility. If chained to fixed bases for refueling, the Pacific Fleet could not have operated much past Midway Island and maintain fuel reserves necessary for combat. It could reach Wake Island only if it had been willing to tow the destroyers back to Hawaii if operations lasted longer than expected. Oilers gave the Pacific Fleet oceanic reach.

While not as critical, the remaining replenishment vessels, the general stores, provisions stores and ammunition ships played an important role in Pacific Fleet plans. They carried supplies, food and ammunition needed for the fleet to fight. The US Navy did not conduct underway replenishment of these in 1941, as the need for replenishment of these items was not as immediate as that of fuel. In 1941, they were intended to be used in advance and unimproved anchorages where they could transfer stores to requisitioning ships. In turn, they were resupplied by the fleet's cargo ships.

The two general issue stores ships and provisions ships carried refrigerated and unrefrigerated dry stores. The two general issue stores ships Castor-class *Castor* and *Pollux*, were new, built in 1939–41 and commissioned by the US Navy in 1941. They displaced 14,400 tons loaded, could carry 4,700DWT of cargo (most of which was refrigerated), were 460ft long, and could steam at 16.5 knots. Three provisions ships, *Bridge*, *Boreas* and *Yukon*, dated to World

Seaplane tenders like *Curtiss* provided a seaplane squadron with everything it needed: fuel, ammunition, maintenance and repair facilities, and sleeping quarters for aircrew. They permitted the Pacific Fleet to set up a seaplane base in any Pacific harbor admitting the tender. (USNHHC)

War I. They were smaller (*Bridge* 424ft long and 8,400 tons displacement; *Boreas* and *Yukon* 416.5ft and 11,570 tons) and slower (14 knots and 11 knots respectively). The fourth, *Aldebaran*, was built in 1938 and similar in capacity and characteristics to *Castor* and *Pollux*. *Bridge* had cargo booms capable of transferring 10 tons; the other three ships had 30-ton booms.

The two ammunition ships, *Pyro* and *Lassen*, resupplied the magazines of the Pacific Fleet's warships. *Pyro* dated to World War I, *Lassen* was new construction. Both were similar in size and performance; 484ft and 459ft long, 14,100 and 14,225 tons displacement, with top speeds of 16 and 15.3 knots respectively. In 1941, they were expected to transfer ammunition in a sheltered anchorage.

There were three different types of support auxiliaries in the US Pacific Fleet: destroyer tenders, submarine tenders and seaplane tenders. The fleet had three destroyer tenders, two submarine tenders and 13 seaplane tenders.

Destroyer tenders maintained and supported destroyers and other small warships. Submarine tenders provided similar services to submarines. Both were equipped with facilities to repair and service critical equipment on the vessels they supported. Facilities included a foundry, a large machine shop, and electrical shops and shops for repairing and servicing anything that could go wrong on destroyers or submarines. Both had shops for servicing torpedoes. They had a sick bay, operating room and dentist's office for the medical needs of the men aboard their vessels.

This was necessary because submarines, destroyers and smaller surface warships lacked the space for these facilities, except on the most rudimentary level. While major naval ports provided these services, such ports were scarce west of Pearl Harbor. Destroyer and submarine tenders served as mobile maintenance facilities that could move to and operate from unimproved anchorages.

All five destroyer and submarine tenders were good-size ships. The smallest, destroyer tender *Dixie*, was 405ft long and displaced 6,114 tons. The rest were 483 to 529ft long and displaced 8,325 to 9,250 tons. The destroyer tenders *Dixie*, *Dobbin* and *Whitney* dated to World War I. The submarine tenders *Fulton* and *Pelias* were new construction built in 1939. There was generally one tender per destroyer or submarine flotilla.

The seaplane tenders served a similar function for the Pacific Fleet's Scouting Force, Aircraft. This consisted of three patrol wings, each with three or four squadrons of Catalina seaplanes. Tenders provided fuel and servicing for the seaplanes using them. Most had cranes to hoist seaplanes aboard for comprehensive maintenance, up to and including engine overhauls, and major repairs.

Seaplane tenders were in essence, mobile seaplane bases. They could set up in a lagoon large enough for a seaplane to take off from and provide everything needed to operate a squadron: fuel, munition, servicing, an operations planning room and living quarters for the flight crew. (Unlike destroyers and submarines no one lived on seaplanes.) This allowed the "eyes of the fleet" (as the seaplanes served) to reach farther than they otherwise could.

US PACIFIC FLEET OPERATIONS IN 1941

The US Pacific Fleet had three seaplane tenders (*Wright, Curtiss, Tangier*), six seaplane tenders, destroyers (AVDs) (*Hulbert, Ballard, Thornton, McFarland, Williamson, Gillis*) and four small seaplane tenders (*Teal, Pelican, Avocet, Swan* and later *Casco*). *Wright* was built in 1920, while *Curtiss, Tangier* and *Casco* were new construction built 1938–40. The rest were World War I warship conversions.

Seaplane tenders, like destroyer and submarine tenders, were large ships, 12,000 to 14,200 tons displacement, ranging in length from 448 to 527ft. They had a top speed of 15 to 19.7 knots. They were capable of supporting an entire patrol wing, if necessary. The small seaplane tenders were Lapwing-class minesweepers converted to seaplane duty. All were converted in the 1930s as the US Navy increased its patrol wings. They were supposed to support a six-plane patrol squadron, but were too small and slow to fill that role satisfactorily.

A better conversion was the seaplane tender, destroyer (AVD). These were Clemson-class destroyers converted by removing the forward two boilers, torpedo tubes and most main guns, and replacing them with aircrew living quarters, aviation fuel storage and aircraft handing equipment. The first conversion was made in 1938 and included *Williamson*. The AVDs proved well suited for this duty, and the US Navy converted another dozen Clemson-class destroyers to seaplane tenders. Each AVD easily maintained a six-Catalina flight at a remote station for extended periods.

The conversions displaced 1,900 tons, and were 311ft long. Even with two boilers, they made 27.5 knots after conversion. Their performance so pleased the US Navy, it ordered construction of a similar-length seaplane tender design in 1939 to overcome the limited number of destroyers available for conversion. One of the first of these Barnegat-class small seaplane tenders, *Casco* was completed at Puget Sound Navy Yard in Bremerton, Washington, and joined the US Pacific Fleet immediately upon commissioning on December 27, 1941.

The final category consisted of vessels that provided services found at a naval base. These included hospital ships, repair ships, rescue and salvage ships, miscellaneous auxiliaries and fleet tugs. They carried the repair capabilities of a developed port to unimproved harbors, including the ability to conduct substantive repairs. While they were normally stationed at Pearl Harbor or West Coast naval ports, they could move to an advance base when called upon. In 1941, the US Pacific Fleet had one hospital ship (*Solace*), three repair ships (*Medusa, Vestal, Rigel*) six fleet tugs, and *ARD-1*, a floating dry dock.

Solace was a civilian passenger liner purchased by the US Navy and converted to a hospital ship. It had

ARD-1, commissioned in 1935, was the third floating dry dock built for the Navy, the first designed to be mobile, and the first of many the US Navy used in the Pacific. At Pearl Harbor on December 7, it ended the war at Kerama Retto. (USNHHC)

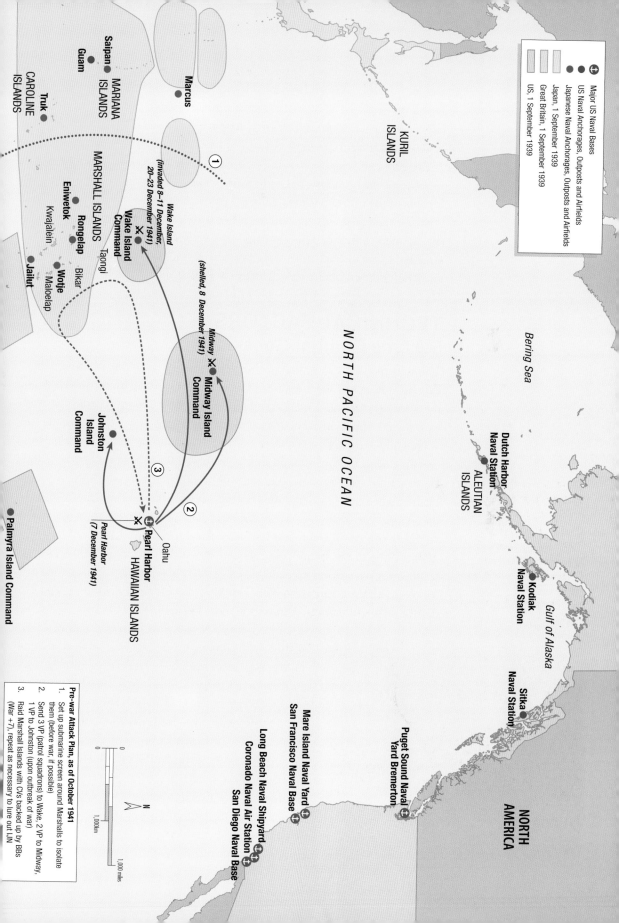

NORTH PACIFIC OCEAN

KURIL
ISLANDS

Bering Sea

Gulf of Alaska

Dutch Harbor
Naval Station
ALEUTIAN
ISLANDS

Kodiak
Naval Station

Sitka
Naval Station

Puget Sound Naval
Yard Bremerton

NORTH
AMERICA

Mare Island Naval Yard
San Francisco Naval Base

Long Beach Naval Shipyard
Coronado Naval Air Station
San Diego Naval Base

Saipan
Guam
Marcus
MARIANA
ISLANDS

Truk
CAROLINE
ISLANDS

MARSHALL ISLANDS

Eniwetok
Rongelap
Kwajalein
Wotje
Maloelap
Jaluit
Bikar
Taongi

Wake Island
Command

① Wake Island
(invaded 8–11 December,
20–23 December 1941)

Midway Island
Command
Midway
(shelled, 8 December 1941)

Johnston
Island
Command

③

②

Oahu
Pearl Harbor
HAWAIIAN ISLANDS
Pearl Harbor
(7 December 1941)

Palmyra Island Command

Pre-war Attack Plan, as of October 1941

1. Set up submarine screen around Marshalls to isolate them (before war, if possible)
2. Send 3 VP (patrol squadrons) to Wake, 2 VP to Midway, 1 VP to Johnston (upon outbreak of war)
3. Raid Marshall Islands with CVs backed up by BBs (War +7), repeat as necessary to lure out IJN

N

0   1,000km
0   1,000 miles

facilities for 461 patients. *Medusa* was built as a repair ship in the 1920s. *Vestal* and *Rigel* were converted from a collier and destroyer tender respectively. They served many of the same maintenance functions as destroyer tenders, but for larger ships. All four ships were large vessels, 8,000 to 12,000 tons, and capable of steaming at 12 to 14 knots.

The fleet tugs were smaller, 1,200 to 1,675tons, and 156 to 205ft long. They were slow, with top speeds of 10 to 16 knots. They were ocean-going tugs, capable of towing vessels much larger than themselves.

ARD-1 required towing, but could operate anywhere. It was the first of the US Navy's mobile floating dry docks used during World War II. While auxiliaries were unglamorous, they gave the US Pacific Fleet the ability to create an advanced port facility anywhere in the Pacific.

TECHNICAL FACTORS
Surface Combat Guns

Through the late 1930s, the US Navy emphasized gunnery. From its earliest days, its power was expressed through the weight of metal of its broadsides and the accuracy of its artillery. Throughout its history, it had equipped its warships with the maximum number of guns of the largest possible (or permissible) size.

The ships of the US Pacific Fleet reflected that tradition, and its battleships and cruisers carried the largest main and secondary guns available at the time of their construction. Even the retrograde step of building cruisers with 6in. instead of 8in. main batteries largely resulted from treaty limitations rather than a desire by the US Navy to abandon the heavy cruiser. The US Navy was the only navy to complete and commission new heavy cruisers during World War II.

Starting with the New York class laid down in 1912 and ending with the California class authorized in 1915, US battleships mounted 14in. guns, while subsequent classes had 16in. main batteries. The older Pacific Fleet battleships carried a 14in./45cal gun. The newer 14in. battleship used the 14in./50cal gun while the fleet's 16in. battleships were equipped with 16in./45cal guns.

The 14in./50cal Mark 10 guns of the battleship *California*. The US Navy prized big guns and was built around a battle line of warships carrying 14in. and 16in. guns. This gun could send a 1,500lb armor-piercing round 38,800 yards down range. (USNHHC)

Applied to guns with a bore greater than 1in., caliber measured the length of the barrel relative to the bore. A 14in./45cal gun had a barrel 45 times longer than the 14in. bore or 52.5ft (630in.) long. Increasing the caliber improved accuracy and permitted a higher muzzle velocity which yielded greater kinetic energy with the same projectile. (For guns with a bore less than 1in., caliber referred to the ratio between the gun's bore and 1in. A .50cal machine gun had a 0.5in. bore.)

The guns carried by Pacific Fleet battleships in 1941 were not the guns installed when the battleships were first built. They had been replaced by improved versions which fired heavier shells with larger charges. Main guns on treaty cruisers were new designs, dating from the 1920s in the Omaha-class 6in./50cal and the 8in./55cal guns used on the treaty heavy cruisers. The Navy designed improved versions of the 6in. and 8in. in the early 1930s that were used in later generations of light and heavy cruisers.

These guns were designed to fight long-range surface actions. Until the advent of radar-laid guns in 1943–44, this meant daytime surface engagements. Yet they were largely used in short-range night actions, where torpedoes frequently dominated. The battleships of the 1941 Pacific Fleet participated in just one long-range gunnery battle during the Pacific War, fought at night. Besides participating in that action, its cruisers fought only one daytime surface action.

UNITED STATES NAVY GUNS

Type	Used on	Year introduced	Rate of fire (rounds per minute)	Projectile type and weight (lbs)	Bursting charge (lbs)	Propellant charge (lbs)	Max range (yards)
16in./45cal Mark 5	Colorado class	1938	1.5	AP: 2,240 HC: 1,900	AP: 33.6 HC: 153.6	Full: 545.0 Reduced: 295.0	35,000
14in./50cal Mark 11	New Mexico class Tennessee class	1935	1.75	AP : 1,500 HC: 1,275	AP: 22.90 HC: 104.21	Full: 420 Reduced:195	36,800
14in./45cal Mark 10	Pennsylvania class Nevada class	1933	1.5–1.75	AP: 1,500 HC: 1,275	AP: 22.90 HC: 104.21	Full: 420 Reduced:205	34,300
8in./55cal Mark 12	San Francisco (late New Orleans class)	1939	3–4	AP: 260 SP Common: 260 HC: 260	AP: 3.64 SP Common: 10.38 HC: 21.37	Full: 85 Reduced: 55	31,860
8in./55cal Mark 11	Early New Orleans class Portland class Indianapolis class Northampton class Pensacola class	1927	3–4	AP: 260 SP Common: 260 Common: 260 HC: 260	AP Mark 19: 3.64 SP Common: 10.38 Common: 10.91 HC: 21.37	Full: 89 Reduced: 44.5	31,860
6in./47cal Mark 16	Brooklyn class St Louis class	1937	8–10	Common: 105 Illum: 94.5	Common: 5.72	Full: 33 Reduced: 21	23,483
6in./53cal Marks 12, 14, 15, 18	Omaha class Argonaut class Nautilus class	1923	6–7	SP Common: 105 Common: 105 HC: 105 Illum: 95.40	SP Common: 2.50 Common: 7.08 HC: 13.22	Standard: 44	25,300
5in./38cal Mark 12	All destroyers after 1933 Yorktown class St Louis class and later	1934	15–22	AA: 55.18 Common: 54.0 SC: 55.18 Illum: 54.39	AA: 7.25 Common: 2.58 SC: 2.04	Full: 15.2-15.5 Reduced: 3.6	17,575
5in./25cal Marks 10, 11, 13	All battleships Lexington class Pensacola class Northampton class New Orleans class Portland class Brooklyn class	1926	15–20	HC: 53.85 AA: 54.0 or 53.8 Illum: 54.5	HC: NA AA: 7.33 or 7.25	9.6*	14,500
5in./51cal Mark 8	All battleships	1911	8–9	Common: 50 HC: 50.0 Illum: 54.5	Common: 1.73 HC: 3.65	Full: 25.0 Reduced: 15.5	16,000
4in./50cal Mark 9	Clemson class Wickes class (and conversions)	1910	8–9	Common: 33.0 SP Common: 33.0 HC: 33.0 Illum 14: 34.66	Common: 1.39 SP Common: 1.16 HC: 2.71	14.5*	15,000
3in./50cal Marks 10, 17, 18, 20	Most submarines (Marks 17 and 18) Auxiliaries	1914	15–20	AP: 13.1 HC: 13 AA: 13 Illum: 13	AP 2: 0.3 HC: 0.74 AA: 0.74	3.7*	14,600
3in./23.5cal Mark 14	Older submarines Auxiliaries Clemson class Wickes class	1913	8–9	Common: 13 AA: 13 Illum: 13	AP 2: 0.28 AA: 0.74	1.23*	10,100

* Unitary projectile and charge

The US Navy's torpedoes were among the world's worst. US submarine torpedo problems are well known, but destroyer and aerial torpedoes also had issues. This Mark 13 aerial torpedo dropped by a Devastator could be released no higher than 50ft and no faster than 110 knots. (USNHHC)

Torpedoes

In 1941, the US Navy's torpedoes may not have been the world's worst, but they came close. They carried a smaller warhead than torpedoes of the Royal Navy, Imperial Japanese Navy and Kriegsmarine (40 percent smaller than Royal Navy torpedoes, half that of Japanese torpedoes, and 5/6th the weight of Kriegsmarine warheads). They had significantly shorter range at the same speed than did British, Japanese and German torpedoes. They also had slower top speeds than torpedoes of other nations.

US torpedoes also ran deep, typically 10ft deeper than set, and were cursed with faulty exploders. To compensate for the small warhead, US torpedoes were fitted with magnetic exploders intended to set off the warhead under the target ship, breaking the keel, but the magnetic exploder could not be made to work, even when the torpedoes did not run deep. The contact exploder was flawed, too. If the striker pin hit dead on, it broke, preventing it from detonating the warhead. (An angled hit reduced the striking force, permitting it to fire, making failures maddeningly inconsistent.)

While some testing problems were the result of government parsimony, others were due to the Navy's sourcing of torpedoes. All were built at one Navy-owned facility, the Newport Torpedo Station. Established in 1907 to build torpedoes, it had a monopoly on torpedo construction from 1920 to 1942. It acquired a monopolistic attitude, in which seniority was more important than ability, and innovation and cost-cutting were discouraged.

The factory was critically important to the Newport, Rhode Island economy. Newport and all of Rhode Island's Congressional delegation were more interested in it as a source of jobs than as a source of weapons critical to the Navy. Incompetent employees could be fired only at the risk of incurring Congressional wrath. The delegation also blocked the Navy from opening torpedo factories elsewhere or contracting with commercial firms for torpedoes.

The torpedo's flaws only emerged in combat as it had not undergone live-fire testing. The magnetic exploder was a closely held secret, locked away, to be released only once war started. No one knew how to use it. The users' manual was kept in a safe.

In 1941, the US Navy had three different torpedoes: the Mark 13, the Mark 14 and the Mark 15. The Mark 13 was an aerial torpedo which entered service in 1938. It was short and fatter than submarine and destroyer torpedoes, with a 22.4in. diameter. It had a 404lb warhead, a top speed of 33 knots and a maximum range of 5,700 yards at 30 knots. It could be dropped no higher than 50ft above water and no faster than 110 knots without risk of breaking up or running wild. In 1941, the Mark 14 was the submarine torpedo in service and the Mark 15, the destroyer torpedo. Both had a 21in. diameter. They entered service in 1931 and 1935 respectively. The Mark 15 was 2ft 1in. longer than the Mark 14's 20ft 6in. length. In 1941, the Mark 14 could travel 4,500 yards at 46 knots or 9,000 yards at 31 knots. Its warhead was 507lb of TNT. The Mark 15 went 6,000 yards at 45 knots or 10,000 yards at 33.5 knots. It carried a warhead of 494lb of TNT.

Antiaircraft Guns

Ships of the US Pacific Fleet were equipped with four heavy antiaircraft guns (5in./38cal, 5in./25cal, 3in./50cal, 3in./23cal) and three medium and light antiaircraft guns (1.1in./75cal, 0.50cal machine gun and 0.30cal machine gun). The heavy antiaircraft guns, especially the 5in./38cal but not the 3in./23cal, were among the best in the world. The lighter antiaircraft guns proved inadequate against 1940s aircraft. They were largely replaced by the end of 1942, but the process had already started in 1941.

Postwar stereotypes held that the US Navy took the threat posed by aircraft lightly before Pearl Harbor, but the reality was different. The Navy converted existing low-powered 3in./23cal from a boat and landing gun to an antiaircraft gun just before World War I by placing it on a high-elevation mount. It only had an 18,000ft ceiling, but that was overkill when introduced in 1913 and through World War I.

During World War I, the Navy developed a high-elevation mount for the existing 3in./50cal, allowing it to be used as an antiaircraft weapon. With a much higher muzzle velocity, it had greater hitting power and an antiaircraft ceiling of 29,000ft. By the 1920s, these formed the main antiaircraft defense for US battleships, with six to ten carried. Both 3in. guns carried a unitary shell and cartridge.

In 1921, the Navy sought a more powerful gun for future use. Using the low-angle 5in./51cal gun as a starting point, it developed a light version. The barrel was shortened to 25cal, allowing it to be moved rapidly. It had a much lower muzzle velocity than the 5in./51cal, and its ceiling was 27,400ft at maximum elevation. These guns formed the heavy antiaircraft battery on treaty cruisers and early aircraft carriers. They replaced 3in./50cal batteries on Pacific Fleet battleships during their late 1920s and early 1930s refits. Battleship antiaircraft batteries were increased to 12 5in./25cal guns.

By 1930, the Navy was developing new destroyer designs. Planners wanted a dual-purpose main gun that could be used against ships and aircraft. The 5in./25cal proved a fine antiaircraft gun and was accurate against

The US Navy had the world's best heavy anti-aircraft guns. Its 5in./25cal guns (firing here) and the 5in./38cal guns that replaced them were effective against both aircraft and ground targets. It proved the right weapon for the Pacific War. (USNHHC)

surface targets, but it lacked the punch of the 5in./51cal. A 38cal version of the 5in. gun was developed.

Its performance was superior to both older 5in. guns. Its rate of fire was much higher than the 5in./51cal, with comparable penetration and range, and it had a 37,200ft ceiling. It was installed on all destroyers from the Farragut class on, all cruisers from the St Louis class, all aircraft carriers starting with the *Yorktown*, and all battleships built after 1935. In 1942, the 5in./38cal gun replaced 5in./25cal guns whenever warships with the older 5in. went through a major rebuild or overhaul.

The weak spot for the Pacific Fleet in 1941 was its light antiaircraft guns, which were the wretched 1.1in./75cal, .50cal and .30cal machine guns. The 1.1in. looked impressive, gaining the nickname "Chicago piano", yet it was mechanically complicated, had a modest rate of fire, and jammed easily. Too slow for "last-ditch" close-in protection against air attack, its shells were too small for intermediate range. It was quickly replaced. In addition, the .50cal and .30cal machine guns were too light for 1940s aircraft.

ANTIAIRCRAFT DOCTRINE IN 1941

There was a mixture of good and bad news when it came to the antiaircraft doctrine of the US Pacific Fleet in 1941. The bad news was there were not enough light antiaircraft guns and even if there had been more, the light antiaircraft guns mounted – .50cal machine guns and 1.1in. "Chicago pianos" – were inadequate. They would be replaced in 1942–43 with the far superior Oerlikon 20mm and Bofors 40mm cannon. Also, tactical response to immediate aerial response was flawed.

The good news was Pacific ships had two of the best heavy antiaircraft weapons of World War II: the superlative 5in./38cal and the slightly less capable 5in./25cal dual-purpose guns. There was also good doctrine when it came to antiaircraft formation. This diagram shows both the antiaircraft formation and how it was used in response to an aerial attack.

The top part shows the antiaircraft formation used, with the carrier in the center, the cruisers around it and the destroyers on the outer perimeter. This took advantage of US strength in heavy antiaircraft guns. The destroyers mounted four to eight 5in./38cal guns, the cruisers eight 5in. guns and the carrier eight or 12 5in. guns. These were 5in./25cal on the older vessels and 5in./38cal on the newer ones. Approaching aircraft encountered two rings of 5in. fire before reaching the carrier and a final barrage before attacking it.

A Combat Air Patrol (CAP) of four or eight Wildcats was maintained over the task force, as an initial line of defense. They typically operated outside the range of the antiaircraft guns, to reduce an attacking force before it reached the task force. By 1941, all Pacific carriers had CXAM radar, which provided a 15- to 25-minute attack warning. This was used to alert the antiaircraft gunners and direct CAP to intercept attacking aircraft.

What happened when an attack occurred is shown on the bottom, in this case an attack by *a rikko* formation of G4M long-range bombers. After radar detects incoming enemy aircraft, CAP is sent to intercept them as they near the formation. Since Japanese aircraft are fragile, CAP shoots down several before they reach the formation, breaking away as they near antiaircraft range. Antiaircraft fire begins as enemy aircraft approach the formation, shooting down one and damaging others. To throw off the aim of the aircrew, ships begin maneuvering independently and randomly as the aircraft near their bomb drop point.

While independent evasion did throw off attackers' aim, it also degraded antiaircraft gun performance. Combat experience, especially in the Far East in January to March 1942, revealed this to be useful only when the ships under attack had weak or no antiaircraft batteries. However, this diagram depicts the doctrine used in 1941.

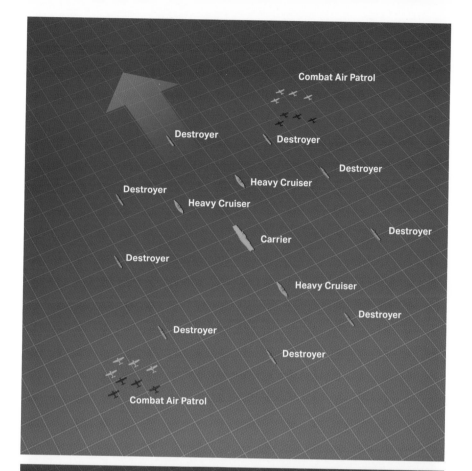

Combat Air Patrol

Destroyer   Destroyer

                              Destroyer

Destroyer   Heavy Cruiser

Destroyer   Heavy Cruiser

                    Carrier   Destroyer

Destroyer

                    Heavy Cruiser

                              Destroyer

          Destroyer

                    Destroyer

Combat Air Patrol

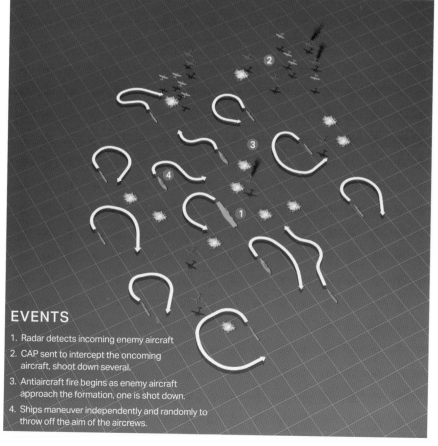

EVENTS

1. Radar detects incoming enemy aircraft

2. CAP sent to intercept the oncoming aircraft, shoot down several.

3. Antiaircraft fire begins as enemy aircraft approach the formation, one is shot down.

4. Ships maneuver independently and randomly to throw off the aim of the aircrews.

Radar

The US Navy began radar development in the mid-1930s. (This was independent of British efforts.) Experimental units were installed in two battleships in late 1938, but a production model radar, CXAM, did not enter service until May 1940. Six CXAM units were installed aboard *California, Yorktown, Pensacola, Northampton, Chester* and *Chicago* in July and August 1940. All were ships in the Pacific Fleet. CXAM detected large warships at 16nm, destroyers at 12nm, multi-engine aircraft flying at 10,000ft at 70nm, and single-engine aircraft at 50nm. (At 1941 aircraft speeds this gave 15–25 minutes' warning.)

An improved version, CXAM-1, arrived in 1941. It offered improved reliability and greater accuracy, reducing uncertainty from 300–400 yards to 200 yards, almost good enough for radar-controlled gunnery. By the end of 1941, six of the 14 warships fitted with CXAM-1 belonged to the US Pacific Fleet: aircraft carriers *Lexington, Saratoga* and *Enterprise*, battleships *Pennsylvania* and *West Virginia*, and seaplane tender *Curtiss*. (The last probably reflected the perceived importance of seaplane tenders.)

These units were large, weighing 5,000lb installed, of which the antennae contributed 1,200lb. This made it impossible to install on ships smaller than a cruiser. The real problem in 1941 was ineffective radar doctrine. How radar was used was as important as its capabilities. In 1941, the Pacific Fleet was still developing its radar doctrine, and by December it remained imperfect. Six of the fleet's 12 radar-equipped warships were at or near Pearl Harbor on December 7. None (including two cruisers at sea, exercising off Oahu) detected the incoming Japanese aircraft.

Aircraft

In 1941, the US Pacific Fleet had roughly 850 aircraft. The number fluctuated throughout the year. Roughly one-tenth of these were trainers, transports or liaison aircraft, and the rest were combat aircraft, including obsolescent types and observation aircraft with limited combat potential. If patrol aircraft were included, the Pacific Fleet had 380 first-line combat aircraft. There were also 120-odd fighters and bombers of obsolescent designs whose main role in the Pacific War was as targets for Japanese warplanes. Another 170 single-engine floatplanes operated from battleships and cruisers.

The Pacific Fleet used three broad categories of aircraft: purely land-based, carrier-based, and floatplanes/amphibians. Under an agreement with the Army Air Force, the US Navy had no purely land-based warplanes in 1941, and Navy aircraft in that category were either trainers or transports, which included multi-engine aircraft. Carrier aircraft could operate off either aircraft

The Brewster Buffalo, the US Navy's first all-metal monoplane fighter, entered service in April 1939. Obsolescent by 1941, it was replaced by the F4F Wildcat. On December 7, the *Lexington*'s Fighting Squadron 2 still flew Buffaloes. (USNHHC)

carriers or airfields. In 1941, all were single-engine aircraft. This included fighters, dive-bombers, torpedo bombers and observation/utility aircraft. Seaplanes fell into two categories: single-engine floatplanes and multi-engine patrol craft.

Fighters defended the carriers and their aircraft. Dive-bombers bombed enemy warships. Torpedo bombers dropped aerial torpedoes. Ideally, a carrier's air group was divided into roughly equal thirds of fighters, dive-bombers and torpedo bombers, but there were too few torpedo bombers available. The shortage was made up by adding dive-bombers, resulting in a ratio of three fighters to four dive-bombers to two torpedo bombers.

In peacetime, including 1941, carriers also held a number of utility aircraft. On December 7, 1941, *Saratoga's* 88-aircraft air group included 20 utility types. These were landed after war broke out to make room for more fighters and bombers.

The US Navy used two fighters in 1941: the F2A Brewster Buffalo and the F4F Grumman Wildcat. Both were aluminum-framed monoplanes with retractable landing gear and closed cockpits. Both carried four 0.50cal machine guns and used the same 1,200hp engine. The Buffalo was older, entering service in April 1939 as the US Navy's first monoplane fighter. The Wildcat, which followed in December 1940, was the superior aircraft. While both were inferior to the A6M Zero, the Wildcat could hold its own, while the Buffalo could not. Also, the Buffalo's engines overheated easily. Wildcats were replacing Buffaloes aboard carriers in 1941, a process completed only by January 1942. Buffaloes were transferred to Marine squadrons operating off island airfields.

The Pacific Fleet used two scout bombers in 1941: the Vought SB2U Vindicator and the Douglas SBD Dauntless. Both were aluminum monoplanes with retractable landing gear and enclosed cockpits. The Vindicator, a revolutionary aircraft when it entered service in 1937, was obsolescent by 1941. It was slower, had a lower service ceiling and shorter range than the Dauntless while carrying half the bombload. The Dauntless dived at a steeper angle. The Dauntless, introduced in 1940, replaced the Vindicator on carriers by mid-1941, with the Vindicator relegated to land-based Marine units.

Both were used as both bombers and scouts. The preferred method of attack was dive-bombing, dropping a bomb in as steep a dive as possible. It was highly accurate, and a hit penetrated deep within a ship. The two aircraft also proved effective scouts and patrol aircraft, replacing single-purpose observation aircraft on aircraft carriers. Both carried two fixed forward-firing .50cal machine guns and a rear-facing twin .30cal flexible mount manned by a gunner. The Dauntless doubled with some success as a fighter.

The Navy's only torpedo plane in 1942 was the Douglas TBD Devastator, a metal monoplane with retractable landing gear and an enclosed cockpit. It entered service in 1937, a few months after the Vindicator. While an excellent torpedo bomber in 1937–38, it was obsolescent in 1941. Slow and underpowered by 1941 standards, it was to be replaced in 1942 by the Grumman TBF Avenger. It was crippled by the poor performance of US torpedoes, and extra speed would

The ungainly-looking Consolidated PBY Catalina was the Pacific Fleet's main maritime patrol aircraft. Although it was never used as a day bomber the way Admiral Kimmel wanted, it proved invaluable as a long-range scout, air-sea rescue craft, anti-submarine aircraft and night torpedo bomber. (USNHHC)

help little as it had to make its torpedo run at no greater than 110 knots, while flying straight and level 50ft above the water.

Also carried aboard Pacific Fleet warships were the Curtis SOC Seagull and Vought OS2U Kingfisher. Usually fitted with floats, both were observation aircraft. (The floats could be replaced with fixed landing gear to fly off carriers or airfields.) The Seagull was the Navy's last operational biplane. Introduced in 1934, it served throughout the Pacific War. The Kingfisher, which entered service in 1939, was a monoplane of metal construction.

Neither was fast; both were underpowered. They were lightly armed, carrying a single fixed forward-firing .50cal machine gun and a rear-facing .30cal machine gun in a flexible mount. Both could perform their intended function, providing observation and gunnery spotting for battleships and cruisers. However, daytime surface actions were rare and carrier aircraft conducted scouting, so these aircraft were never used as intended. They proved useful locating and recovering downed aircrew and were retained for that purpose. In 1941, battleships carried Kingfishers, while cruisers carried Seagulls. Treaty cruisers typically carried four floatplanes; battleships and Omaha class carried three.

The final combat aircraft of the 1941 Pacific Fleet was the Consolidated PBY Catalina, a twin-engine flying boat. A parasol-winged monoplane, it entered service in 1936. Slow, with a top speed of 170 knots and a cruising speed of 109 knots, it had an extremely long range, 2,190nm. It had a crew of ten, and carried three .30cal machine guns (two in a nose turret and one in a ventral hatch) and two .50cal machine guns (in port and starboard waist blisters) for defense. It also carried up to 4,000lb in bombs, depth charges and torpedoes. Later versions were amphibian, with retractable landing gear permitting them to operate off water or on airfields.

A multi-purpose aircraft, its primary mission was patrol and reconnaissance. Prewar, the Navy envisioned using it as a long-range strike bomber, primarily employing torpedoes, but it was too slow for mass daylight torpedo runs, so this was never attempted. It proved highly effective as a night torpedo bomber, as an ASW aircraft, and in air-sea rescue, and it was a highly effective long-range patrol aircraft in the Pacific. Its operational flexibility made it one of World War II's most useful aircraft. In 1941, the US Pacific Fleet had 130 Catalinas distributed among ten patrol squadrons.

Men

The equipment a navy has, the ships, guns, torpedoes and aircraft, are hypnotizing. Yet the men manning the ships and operating its weapons are any fleet's most important factor. Without skilled and dedicated men, a navy is worthless. The 1941 Pacific Fleet had professional crews led by competent officers.

The United States Navy was born in 1794 when the United States Congress authorized the creation of a navy. Between 1794 and 1939, it remained a relatively small, highly professional service with a tradition of victory. It had a history of winning small, short wars with existing ships and personnel and an ability to expand rapidly during major conflicts. Although the 1941 US Pacific Fleet included some personnel from the build-up begun in 1939, most of those manning it came from this tradition.

During the 1920s and 1930s, the US Navy relied on long-service sailors in both enlisted and officer ranks. The Depression years of the 1930s, when civilian jobs were scarce, allowed the Navy to be highly selective of those who served, permitting only the best to re-enlist.

The enlisted ranks were men author Richard McKenna (who served in the US Navy at that time) termed "the Sons of Martha." Kipling's poem of that name described them as the ones whose care it is "that the gear engages, the wheels run truly." The description fitted the period's enlisted sailor and his professionalism.

When World War II began in 1939, the Navy changed. The United States remained neutral until December 1941, but anticipated entry. It began expanding the Navy in the late 1930s, including vastly expanded numbers of both enlisted and commissioned personnel. In 1939, the US Navy totalled 125,202 personnel; by 1941, it had increased to 383,150.

Despite this three-fold expansion, enlistment in the US Navy remained voluntary. The Navy maintained higher physical and mental enlistment standards than the United States Army. The Navy was a highly technical service. Navy service offered better living conditions and the opportunity to learn skills that could be transferred to peacetime work.

The prewar officers and men served as a cadre for the wartime Navy with its reserve officers and wartime enlistees. Even by December 1941, regular officers provided a preponderance of the US Pacific Fleet's leadership. At least half of its enlisted strength, including a vast majority of its petty officers, was made up of regular sailors, not wartime enlistees.

Training was a continuous process in the US Navy. It began when an individual entered the service, and ended when he left. All men enlisting in the Navy began their careers at Navy Boot Camp. (Except for nurses, the US Navy was all male in 1941.)

Recruits attended one of four boot camps (San Diego, California; Bainbridge, Maryland; Newport, Rhode Island; and Great Lakes, Illinois). There, recruits were issued their uniform and kit (including a copy of the Bluejacket's Manual) and learned the fundamentals of being a sailor: basic drill, seamanship, naval customs and courtesy, small arms training, swimming, and how to live aboard ship.

Upon graduation, new seamen were either assigned directly to ships (where they learned their duties essentially

The Patten brothers were typical of the men who made up the enlisted ranks of the Pacific Fleet in 1941. Iowa farmboys, they joined the Navy for a steady job. These seven brothers, Ted, Gilbert, Marvin, Bick, Allen, Bub and Bruce Patten served in *Nevada*'s engine room. (USNHHC)

through an apprenticeship), or to a school (where they received specialty training). There were three categories of schools. Class-A schools provided elementary instruction in technical fields and gave recruits the groundwork to move into the lowest petty-officer ratings. These included a broad range of specialties – electrical, ordnance, communications, clerical, machinists, metalworkers, woodworkers, radiomen, diesel engine mechanics, hospital corpsmen, even bugling.

Class-B schools gave enlisted men more advanced instruction. This included courses in advanced machinery such as bombsights, optics or gyro compasses, firefighting, or torpedoman training. Men attending these schools had some navy experience, and in 1941 were not raw recruits. Class-C schools were more advanced still, providing training in subjects not normally a part of shipboard instruction. Men accepted into them were either in the top tier of their Class-A school or showed superior capability during sea service.

The system worked well. Operating a ship required many specialized skills; it also needed much unskilled labor. The Navy's long tradition of on-the-job training had sailors "striking" (training for) more skilled positions than their current assignment while at sea. Recruits did necessary unskilled work upon arriving at their ships, at the guns, in the machinery rooms, or as part of the deck crew. They learned additional skills serving on their ship.

Prewar and during the war's opening year, the US Navy was rigidly segregated. Blacks and Asians (especially Chinese and Filipinos) could only serve as messmen or stewards. (Hispanics and Native Americans were largely treated as "white" for service purposes.)

In 1941, the US Navy's officers were mostly long-serving, professional officers. Many were graduates of the United States Naval Academy at Annapolis, Maryland. These men had gone through a four-year training period, including a college education and summer cruises. Officers were expected to be gentlemen as well as mariners. The US Navy expected gentlemen to have a college education, and serve as leaders.

When the Navy began growing in 1935, its leaders realized this officer corps was too small for the intended growth. The Navy initiated a Reserve Officer Training School (ROTC) system at US colleges and universities, where students received naval training along with their baccalaureate degrees, gaining a reserve commission upon graduation. This included men at maritime academies intending to serve as merchant marine officers.

During World War II, ROTC training was vastly expanded, including the creation of the V-7 program in June 1940. V-7 candidates attended college, completed an eight-month course at the United States Naval Reserve Midshipmen's School, and were given an ensign's commission upon graduation. The V-7 program was intended to create 36,000 officers. Others officers were appointed directly from civilian life, including many with prewar college degrees who had gone through Reserve Officer training. (Some received rapid promotion based on their existing experience and skills.)

HOW THE FLEET OPERATED

DOCTRINE AND COMMAND

When created, the US Pacific Fleet was an Admiral's slot. Whichever officer held the command received a temporary promotion to four-star rank, regardless of his permanent rank. The fleet was divided into four "forces": Battle Force, Scouting Force, Base Force and Amphibious Force. The first two were Vice Admiral (three-star) commands; the last two commanded respectively by a Rear Admiral and a Major General (two-star). The fleet was supported by five Naval Districts, responsible for naval coastal frontier defense and operation of the associated navy yard, bases and air stations. These were the 11th Naval District (California south of Point Arguello), 12th Naval District (California north of Point Arguello), 13th Naval District (Washington, Oregon, Alaska Territory), 14th Naval District (Pacific Fleet Operational Control: Hawaii and island commands) and 15th Naval District (Canal Zone).

Battle Force, Pacific Fleet contained all of the Pacific Fleet's battleships, aircraft carriers (and carrier aircraft), light cruisers and destroyers. There were three three-ship battleship divisions, two carrier divisions, two light cruiser divisions and 11 four-ship destroyer divisions. It also contained Minecraft, Battle Force, which had two mine squadrons, one with two divisions of minelayers, and one with three divisions of fast minesweepers.

Eleven Pacific Fleet battleships steam in formation. For many in the 1941 US Pacific Fleet, the battleship *was* the fleet, the reason for its existence and its main offensive punch. Prewar plans focused on ways to bring the battle line into combat. (USNHHC)

Husband Kimmel jumped over the heads of 46 more senior officers to command the US Pacific Fleet. A battleship admiral, he was viewed as the right man for the job by admirals with extensive aircraft and submarine experience. He retained command for only ten months. (USNHHC)

It was intended to operate as a unit, centered on a battle line of nine to 12 battleships facing an enemy battle line. The light cruisers and destroyers protected the battleships from torpedo attack. The light cruisers especially, with their spray of 6in. shells, were supposed to cut down the enemy's light cruisers and destroyers before they reached torpedo range. The destroyers awaited opportunities to attack light warships with their guns and make torpedo runs at enemy battleships. The carriers, operating in independent task forces, were to provide scouting with their aircraft to find and fix the enemy.

Scouting Force, Pacific Fleet held all the Pacific Fleet's heavy cruisers, patrol squadrons (VPs with patrol aircraft), and submarines. There were 12 heavy cruisers divided into three four-ship divisions, ten patrol squadrons split among three patrol wings, and five divisions of submarines. Because the function of the force was scouting, they typically did not operate as a unit. Rather, each group operated independently, the cruisers often accompanying Battle Force carrier groups. In the case of the patrol aircraft and submarines, each unit usually operated independently, although their efforts were coordinated.

Base Force, Pacific Fleet provided fleet logistics. It contained auxiliary warships the Pacific Fleet needed to operate in a mobile environment. It was, in essence, a mobile navy base and navy yard, right down to a dry dock. It contained one squadron of repair vessels and seagoing tugs, one squadron of troop transports, a squadron of Bird-class minesweepers, a logistics ship squadron (which included fleet oilers) and a collection of various miscellaneous auxiliaries.

Amphibious Force, Pacific Fleet was a corps-size force of ground troops. It included one US Army infantry division, one Marine division, and various smaller US Marine Corps units, including a Marine air wing and several Marine defense battalions. These troops provided the manpower for the initial phase of planned amphibious landings, and occupation of captured islands.

Leading the Pacific Fleet was Admiral Husband E. Kimmel. A humorless man with little creative spark, he possessed charm and courtesy. He jumped over the heads of 46 senior officers to assume command. When appointed he was viewed as the right man for the job by most officers, including Nimitz and Halsey. He was a surface warship man, having spent his entire seagoing career aboard battleships and destroyers. Kimmel had no exposure to naval aviation. He was extremely aggressive, always seeking ways to engage the enemy.

His three principal subordinates were Vice Admiral William S. Pye commanding Battle Force, Vice Admiral Wilson Brown commanding Scouting Force, and Vice Admiral William S. Halsey commanding Aircraft, Battle Force and holding a second hat commanding Carrier Division 2. All three held temporary ranks of vice admiral due to their assignments. Halsey took command in June 1940 of what was then Aircraft US Fleet, while Pye and Brown assumed their commands when Pacific Fleet was created.

Pye and Brown were both surface warship officers, with extensive battleship and destroyer service. Halsey started out on surface warships, serving aboard battleships, and commanding destroyers, but transferred to naval aviation in 1934. Halsey had more carrier aviation experience than any other senior US Navy officer except Admiral Ernest King (commanding US Atlantic Fleet in 1941).

Pye was as cautious as Kimmel was aggressive. As Kimmel's second in command he was a good foil, tempering Kimmel's manner. Brown and Halsey were more aggressive. Brown proved a bold leader in early 1942, commanding a carrier task force. He was shifted to shore commands in April 1942 due to ill health. Halsey proved the acme of an offensive admiral during the Pacific War.

US Navy war plans against Japan dated from the early 1900s, when Japan emerged as a world power. It was rightly viewed as the United States' primary strategic rival in the Pacific, just as Britain was then viewed as the US's primary strategic rival in the Atlantic. The US view of Britain mellowed after the Anglo-American alliance in World War I, while, because of its continued aggression, Japan was increasingly viewed as a threat.

In the 1920s and 1930s, the US Army and Navy drew up a succession of war plans aimed at Japan, code named "Plan Orange" after the color assigned to Japan. (Plans were drawn up for a potential war with each nation, and each was assigned a color for planning purposes, red [or variations] for Britain and the Commonwealth, black for Germany, orange for Japan, green for Mexico, and so forth. None anticipated US initiation. All were contingencies in the event that war broke out with that nation.)

Plan Orange had multiple variations while in force. Some versions covered only the initial phases of a Pacific war with Japan, outlining plans to secure bases in the Marshall and Caroline Islands, with the rest of the war left to be determined later. Others detailed war plans up to and including capture of the Tsushima Islands and a naval blockade of the Japanese Home Islands.

All had common factors. All included a drive across the Central Pacific. Islands in the Marshall Chain would be taken first, with a forward naval base established at Eniwetok or Wotje. Although early plans posited capturing multiple Marshall Islands, by the late 1930s most would be bypassed, relying on aircraft based on the captured atolls to neutralize Japanese garrisons on uncaptured islands.

Once a base in the Marshalls was secured, an atoll in the Caroline Islands would be taken. Usually, Truk was the target even though US Naval Intelligence believed it to be heavily fortified, "the Gibraltar of the Pacific." Despite that, plans held it could be taken by a reinforced division of Marines or soldiers, by taking lightly held islands in the atoll and using those to neutralize the heavily defended ones. A naval

Rear Admiral William Halsey (center in light-colored coat) poses with his staff aboard USS *Enterprise* in the late fall of 1941. Halsey had more experience with aircraft carriers than anyone else in the Navy save Atlantic Fleet commander Ernest King. (USNHHC)

base would be set up in its lagoon. (Other Caroline atolls were considered as alternatives to Truk. Prewar planners never looked at Ulithi though, which was actually used as a US Navy anchorage and naval base in 1944–45.)

After that, different plans diverged wildly. Some continued the drive west to relieve or recapture the Philippines. From there, Japanese access to the resource-rich South China Sea would be cut off, strangling the Japanese war machine. Others swung north to take the Marianas.

This was not to allow the Marianas to be used as a platform to bomb Japan. In the 1930s, aircraft lacked the range to attack Japan from the Marianas. Rather, it was intended to lure the Japanese fleet into a major naval battle. All Orange Plans anticipated a major naval engagement with Japan west and north of the Caroline–Mariana line. They intended to force a battle in waters distant from the Home Islands. A fight at the Marianas left the Imperial Navy 1,200nm from its bases in Japan, while the US Pacific Fleet could repair and refit at the new base in Truk, only 600nm distant.

All Orange Plans assumed the US and Japan would be the only combatants. Other nations, including European colonial nations – Britain, France and the Netherlands – would remain neutral. Most assumed the US would fight only Japan. (One plan examined the consequence of an Anglo-Japanese alliance against the US. Results convinced planners to strengthen the special relationship between the US and Britain.) Orange Plans also assumed the US Navy could not rely on prewar Far East naval bases. Singapore and the Philippines were judged too vulnerable to Japanese interdiction, so new bases would be built to support the US Pacific Fleet on its westward progression.

The 1939 start of war in Europe ended the single-foe assumption of War Plan Orange. Concurrent wars with Germany and Japan were viewed as almost inevitable. One result was the Two-Ocean Navy Act of 1940, vastly expanding the US Navy. The other was abandonment of individual "color" war plans, combining all into a single, multi-front "Rainbow Plan." It assumed a war with both Germany and Japan.

Five Rainbow Plans were developed. Rainbow One, Two and Four were purely defensive, limited to the Western Hemisphere. Rainbow Three assumed the major effort would be against Japan, essentially following Plan Orange. Rainbow Five was a "Germany first" plan. Adopted in late 1940, it continued to be tweaked until November 1941.

While Rainbow Five gave Germany priority, it only altered Plan Orange in terms of timeline. The Central Pacific drive would still occur, but would be delayed as much as two years. The Army advocated the Navy stand entirely on the defensive, guarding a triangle in the Eastern Pacific formed by the Aleutians, Hawaii and the Canal Zone.

That was further than the Navy was prepared to go. The Chief of Naval Operations, Admiral Harold Stark, told Kimmel to act offensively with the Pacific Fleet. While invasions had to be delayed, raids and active forward defense were encouraged. This was all the permission an aggressive Kimmel was given. The plan he and his operations officer, Captain Charles H. McMorris, drew up remained within Stark's restrictions, while wildly violating its spirit. It offered the Japanese two pieces of bait, Wake Island and the Pacific Fleet's carriers. Kimmel felt either would lure part of Japan's fleet east, where it could be cut off and destroyed by his battle line.

Kimmel had airfields and seaplane bases built on Wake, Midway and Johnston Islands. Wake, 2,000nm west of Pearl Harbor, would house two or three patrol squadrons, a force that would threaten the Northern Marshall Islands. It would be supported by patrol squadrons operating out of Midway. When war started, Battle Force with Scouting Force submarines, would move to cover Wake (six days steaming from Hawaii). A submarine cordon would wear down any Japanese force sent to reduce Wake. Battle Force, led by the battleships, would smash the surviving ships.

If that failed to lure the Japanese to battle, Kimmel's backup was to threaten an invasion in the Marshalls. It would open with carrier raids on Japanese garrisons in the Marshalls. A complex ballet of moving battleships, cruisers and carriers (more complicated than Japan's 1942 Midway invasion plans) would respond to

To provide forward bases to attack the Japanese, Kimmel built fortified bases on Wake, Midway and Johnston Islands during 1941. While incomplete by December, all were capable of operating land-based aircraft and seaplanes by then. This is Midway in November 1941. (USNHHC)

BATTLE PRACTICE (overleaf)

For Husband Kimmel, the ultimate expression of Pacific Fleet power was the battle line, the battleships belonging to Battle Force's battleship divisions. Carriers and cruisers had their place, but to Kimmel that place was supporting the battleships. Although intellectually he understood how powerful naval aircraft had become, he had spent his entire career in surface warships, especially battleships. He viewed leading a line of battleships into combat as a fitting culmination of his career.

Succeeding in battle required skilled crews. This meant constant practice, practice in individual and divisional ship handling and gunnery practice, including live-fire practice. Kimmel trained his battleships hard, including sea practice and gunnery competitions.

This plate shows one such exercise, gunnery practice at sea in the waters off Hawaii in summer 1941. All nine battleships are present. In the lead are the battleships of Battle Division 4, the three Colorado-class ships, with flagship *West Virginia* leading followed by *Maryland* and

Colorado. They are followed by Battle Division 2, *California* (flagship), *Tennessee* and *Nevada*. The rearguard is formed by Battle Division 1, with *Arizona* (flagship), *Pennsylvania* and *Oklahoma*.

This is near the end of the exercise: long-range battle practice, a standard live-fire exercise. Each ship fires at a towed target located at least 17,000ft away. The battleships fire one at a time, so the results can be scored. Long-range battle practice had two objectives: training main battery personnel in long-range fire under day battle conditions and training ships' spotters in target acquisition. (Radar-directed gunfire lay in the near future.) While several broadsides are fired, accuracy and speed are emphasized. Ships are expected to hit and hit early, and ships that got on target rapidly scored higher points.

At the point captured in the plate, *California* has just fired, and *Tennessee* is now firing. *West Virginia*, *Maryland* and *Colorado*, ahead in the line of battle, have already fired, and *Nevada*, *Pennsylvania*, *Arizona* and *Oklahoma* are next.

any Japanese naval retaliation. It was predicated on a naval response. Had Japan responded by reinforcing Marshall Islands air garrisons, the Pacific Fleet's ships (especially the carriers) would be put at risk without a reward to balance the risk.

The Pacific Fleet of 1941 is often criticized for overemphasis of the battle line and neglect of the potential of its aircraft carriers, but this criticism is unfair. The US Navy knew what aircraft carriers could do, based on fleet exercises in the mid-1930s. The problem was the US Navy's limited number of carriers. They had only seven fleet carriers, and two, *Ranger* and *Wasp*, were too small to be used effectively in the Pacific. A massive wave of new construction – the first of the Essex class – was under way, but few new ships would be available until the beginning of 1943.

The alternative to the 1941 Pacific Fleet using the battleship force as its main striking arm was to sit on the defensive until early 1943. Kimmel's plans reflected both his battleship inclinations and the resources available, cutting the fleet's coat to fit the cloth available.

Aircraft potential grew dramatically during the mid and late 1930s, faster than it could be factored into naval planning. In 1935, all carrier aircraft had open cockpits and fixed landing gear, most used wood-and-fabric construction and virtually all were biplanes. By 1940, aluminum monoplanes with retractable landing gear were the norm, and bombloads and guns mounted had more than doubled. It was a quantum growth in striking power. While many admirals (including Halsey and King) understood this, doctrine had not yet caught up with aircraft capabilities.

INTELLIGENCE, DECEPTION, AND COMMUNICATION

The intelligence needed by the US Pacific Fleet can be divided into two broad categories, strategic and operational. Strategic intelligence covered the enemy's capabilities: how many ships, aircraft and bases it had and their weapons, speeds and ranges. Operational intelligence involved the locations of enemy forces and their status. (Tactical intelligence, finding enemy forces to attack them, was generally conducted by scouting units, and the responsibility of individual task forces and groups.)

Responsibility for strategic and operational intelligence was split between the Office of Naval Intelligence (ONI) and the Office of Naval Communications (ONC) Communications Security Group (also known as OP-20-G). Both the ONI and OP-20-G operated out of US Navy headquarters in Washington DC. By 1941, both had sections working within the headquarters of the three US Navy fleets.

The ONI was formed in 1882 to collect and record useful naval information. It is the United States' oldest intelligence gathering

Lieutenant Commander Joseph Rochefort headed OP-20-G's HYPO station. Rochefort, one of the few US Navy officers who spoke and read Japanese, started as an enlisted man. This picture shows him as a lieutenant in 1934, on the staff of Admiral Joseph Reeves, then commanding the US Fleet. (USNHHC)

agency. It was responsible for assessing the capabilities of the world's navies. OP-20-G was founded in 1922 charged with protecting US Navy communications security. Its first director, Laurence Safford, expanded that mandate to include interception, decryption, and analysis of naval communications of foreign nations viewed as likely enemies. Japan was a particular point of focus throughout the 1920s and 1930s.

During World War II, these organizations reached an efficiency rarely achieved in history. In the years between the world wars their performance was less satisfactory. Several factors explain this, especially when gathering intelligence about Japan and the Imperial Japanese Navy.

One reason was ONI and OP-20-G often failed to attract the best officers. Intelligence, codes and signals seemed far removed from most naval officers' career goal: command of a fleet. Some flag officers of that period saw it as a crackpot endeavor and men in those slots as odd. Promotion required sea time, and intelligence postings were shore assignments. Many officers viewed intelligence assignments as career poison if they remained too long.

Few naval officers spoke or read Japanese, almost a necessity for this type of work. Relatively few Japanese immigrated to the United States and racial prejudice prevented those who did from obtaining US Navy commissions in that era. Few Americans took Oriental languages in college. Since the early 1920s, the Navy sent two officers to Japan annually (and one Marine Corps officer every other year) to a three-year language course in Japan. This yielded a handful of Japanese-speaking officers.

Finally, racial prejudice and cultural ignorance played a role. Prior to World War II, Asians were seen as inferior to Europeans. (In fairness, many Asians likewise felt Americans and Europeans to be racially inferior.) This led ONI and OP-20-G to consistently underestimate Japan's capability for innovation and boldness. In many cases, they remained oblivious to Japanese technological advances. Also, US Navy officers did not understand Japanese culture and society. They assumed their Japanese counterparts would have the same motivations and values as any officer from a Western society. In reality, there were important differences.

Despite their shortcomings, the US Navy's intelligence services gave the Pacific Fleet a solid foundation in the field. This was especially true of operational intelligence, which used a combination of radio interception and radio direction finding. Radio stations in Hawaii and the Philippines intercepted Japanese radio traffic, transcribed it and sent it to local OP-20-G offices for decryption. The Hawaii office was codenamed HYPO, the Philippines office, located on Corregidor, codenamed CAST, and the office in Navy Headquarters in Washington DC codenamed NEGAT.

The US Navy also maintained a series of listening posts along the Pacific Coast and throughout the Pacific (including Hawaii, Midway, Guam and the Philippines) that located the direction a Japanese naval radio message came from. By cross-indexing the bearings they could establish a location.

The US Navy cracked the Imperial Navy's operational code (the Red and Blue codes) in the 1920s and was able to read them. The US Army cracked the Japanese diplomatic codes (the Purple Code) and read those. The Navy was unable to read the higher-level JN-25 command code during the 1930s, but had it under cryptographic attack at its Hawaii office. By 1941, HYPO was beginning to unravel it, but could not read messages encoded in it.

However, HYPO could decipher the headers, which revealed the identity of the ship and its location. From that they could piece together the Imperial Navy's order of battle, and its possible intentions. For example, a large collection of warships in Japan's Formosa naval port of Takao (now Kaohsiung in Taiwan), implied a move south to the Dutch East Indies. HYPO got very good at this. During the second half of 1941, it had the location of the Imperial Fleet well defined. The problem was twofold: it used past performance to predict future events and its forecasts depended

LONG-RANGE MARITIME AERIAL RECONNAISSANCE

By 1941, long-range patrol aircraft had largely replaced cruisers as fleet scouts. Aircraft moved faster, 100 knots to a scouting cruiser's 15–20 knots. They could range farther than cruisers. From a perch 3,000 to 7,000 ft above the ocean, they could see a lot farther than cruisers. While they could not scout in bad weather, and had difficulty at night, cruisers were also handicapped by visibility issues. Best of all, scout aircraft numbers were not limited by naval treaties.

The US Navy had large numbers of VP patrol squadrons, and the Pacific Fleet had 11 and plans to use them. The diagram shows how a 12-PBY squadron would be deployed to patrol the ocean, in this example Midway. Nine of the squadron's 12 aircraft are on patrol, with the other three at base for maintenance or repair.

Each PBY is sent out on different headings, 20 degrees apart, in pie-shaped patrol wedges. They fly out around 680nmi, turn left or right, fly another 100nmi, and then return to base. The total distance flown is 1,460 to 1,500nmi, 70 percent of a Catalina's full range. That allows a fuel margin for contingencies (including spotting and trailing enemy ships).

At PBY cruising speeds, each patrol takes 14 hours, close to the daylight period at Midway during summer. (In the winter, it is as short as 10.3 hours.) It is relatively easy to take off in the dark, but difficult (before radar) to land at night, especially on water.

All planes should land before it is fully dark. Nautical twilight adds another hour to the end of the day. Even during summer most patrols will take off before sunrise, reaching their maximum range by late morning to noon, even if takeoffs are staggered. They have to head home seven hours before nautical twilight. In the winter, even in a tropical winter, a pilot will be in the air hours before astronomical twilight.

While the plot seems to show several gaps between patrol routes, they are more apparent than real. A fleet at sea covers a lot of ocean, with a footprint of up to 25 square miles. It produces smoke and wakes in clear weather the PBY's crew can spot 25–30 miles away (the distance of the disc on which the aircraft outline is centered). In the Central Pacific there are many clear days.

Ships, when steaming to conserve fuel, are slow. A transport fleet carrying invading troops travels at 10 knots at most – or 240nm a day. Warships typically cruise at 15 knots, 360nm daily. A high-speed run in at 20 knots (which eats a tremendous amount of fuel) covers 480nm. Even in the best case (for the attacker), they will be spotted at least 200nm from their objective.

While the area patrolled covers an arc of 180 degrees, it is sufficient to cover all areas an enemy is likely to approach from. Steaming to avoid the patrolled area adds over 1,000nm to the trip, even when cutting corners.

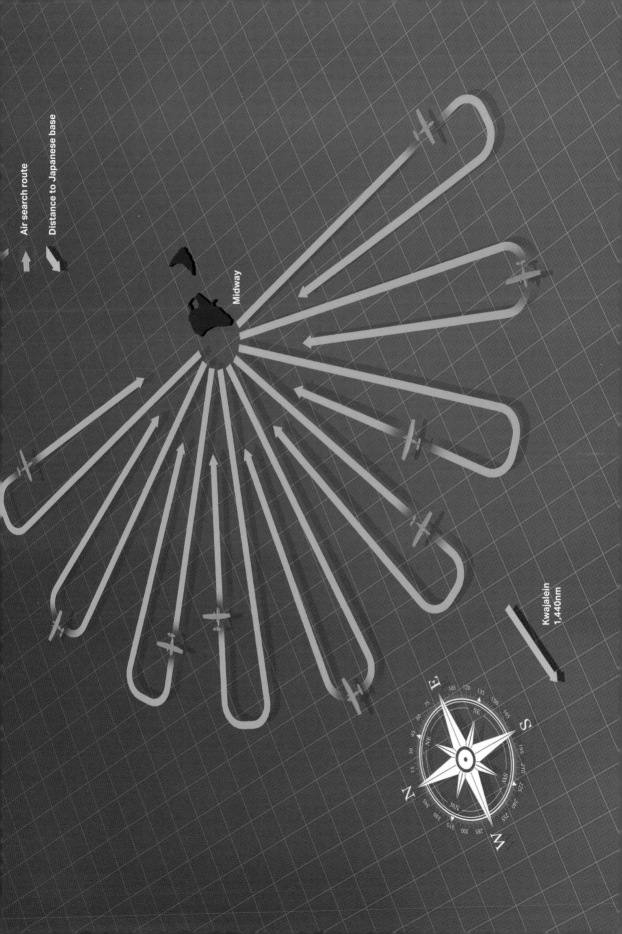

Air search route

Distance to Japanese base

Midway

Kwajalein
1,440nm

Edwin T. Layton was the Pacific Fleet's intelligence officer in 1941. One of the Navy's few Japanese-speaking officers, he gave Kimmel his assessment of the Japanese fleet and its operations. This shows him as a captain in 1944 while serving on Admiral Nimitz's staff. (USNHHC)

on the ships broadcasting radio messages. Mark Twain is reputed to have said: "It ain't what you don't know that gets you into trouble. It's what you know for sure that just ain't so." The aphorism's truth would be demonstrated by the end of December 1941.

Japan pulled the carrier division from three of its five fleets, withdrew two fast battleships, two heavy cruisers and a destroyer division to form a fast carrier attack force, the *Kidō Butai* (Mobile Force). None of these ships changed call signs and the *Kidō Butai* and the fleets from which they were drawn remained in Japan's Inland Sea. The shift went undetected by HYPO's Traffic Analysis team.

Next, the *Kidō Butai* went radio silent in late November. This was done to prevent US radio direction from finding it (the Imperial Navy thought its codes were secure), but it eliminated the radio messages Traffic Analysis needed for their assessments. The carriers disappeared. The signals that were intercepted came from Home waters, although some were inappropriate duplicates of previous messages (sent to maintain traffic volume, again assuming Imperial Navy codes were secure). Lacking other evidence, Pacific Fleet intelligence reluctantly placed the carriers in Home waters.

This was due to intelligence compartmentalization. Various Japanese codes were read by different organizations, and for security reasons they were shared. Each organization had only one piece, and the puzzle could not be solved without putting all the pieces together.

The only deception practiced by the Pacific Fleet was operational deception: arriving suddenly at an unexpected spot or approaching an enemy formation undetected to achieve operational surprise. This was achieved through a number of techniques. One was maintaining radio silence at sea to prevent RDF location finding. During operations, rendezvous times and locations were arranged in advance. This created operational rigidity, but radio silence could be abandoned if circumstances merited.

Another technique used was a high-speed run to a target. This was most often used during a carrier raid or a planned bombardment of an enemy shore installation. A task force or group would make the final run to an objective at two-thirds speed or flank speed, allowing it to cross a danger zone swiftly. Prior to the run, the ships would refuel at sea from oilers at a safe distance from an enemy. After the attack, a high-speed withdrawal, followed by a fresh rendezvous with oilers and refueling would take place.

Communications played an important part in US Pacific Fleet planning and operations. Shipboard radios were common, and each ship had a communications officer. Codes and ciphers played an important role in naval communication, and messages sent and received were routinely enciphered. High-priority messages were enciphered in a special cipher hard to crack, and these had to be deciphered by the communications officer.

Naval aircraft were routinely equipped with radios by 1940, which included voice-radio on VHF frequencies. These could be used in single-seat aircraft, such as fighters, which allowed individual aircraft in a formation to communicate with each other. Both attack and defense could be better coordinated, yielding capabilities undreamed of ten years earlier.

Low frequency to high frequency radio waves reflected off the ionosphere, permitting over-the-horizon communications. VHF was line of sight, which limited range, but this was acceptable as these communications were intended for use over short ranges.

VHF could be used for more than talk between aircraft; it could also be used for real-time voice communications between ships in a formation. Using "talk between ships" (TBS), captains could exchange information, coordinate maneuvers and clarify uncertainties. However, TBS was insecure, permitting an enemy to listen in. It was also short range, impervious to shore-based RDF. Ship-based direction finding was in its infancy in 1941, in the experimental phase in the US Navy and non-existent in the Imperial Navy. On the other hand, the tactical information exchanged over TBS usually lost value too quickly for it to prove useful to eavesdroppers.

LOGISTICS AND FACILITIES

Logistics shaped the US Pacific Fleet. Its crews had to be fed and clothed. Its weapons required ammunition. Its ships required maintenance supplies and had to be fueled. Everything had to be brought from the West Coast to forward bases in the Pacific, and in 1941 Pearl Harbor was the Pacific Fleet's largest forward base.

Logistics were critical because the distances involved in a Pacific War were hemispheric. From California ports to Pearl Harbor was 2,830nm. From Washington State to Pearl Harbor was 3,200nm. Most supply ships steamed at 10 knots, so it took almost two weeks for a cargo departing the West Coast to reach Oahu.

The Philippines was a frequent Plan Orange destination. To reach Manila Bay in the Philippines from Pearl Harbor a ship had to travel another 4,600nm, nearly three weeks by sea. One could go by air. Pan American Airlines had a flying boat service from San Francisco to Manila. It stopped at Hawaii, Midway, Wake Island and Guam (1,500nm from Wake), before making the final 1,600nm flight to Manila. The Boeing 377 had a cruising speed of 155 knots, which gave a total flight time of 51 hours, including a 19-hour nonstop flight to Hawaii. With overnight stops the trip was five days.

Pacific distances meant fuel consumption drove everything. Auxiliaries, like the fleet oiler USS *Neosho* (AO-22), permitted refueling at sea while under way. It gave the Pacific Fleet the legs it needed to take the war to the enemy. (USNHHC)

Distances to US naval stations in the Pacific from Pearl Harbor were formidable, if not as long. From Pearl Harbor it was 1,997nm to Wake Island, 1,463 to Midway, 954 to Johnston Atoll and 959 to Palmyra Atoll. It was 3,300nm to steam directly from Pearl Harbor to American-held Guam in the otherwise Japanese-controlled Marianas Islands. Except for Guam, Pearl Harbor remained the closest US naval base to these naval stations. (Guam was 1,600nm from Subic Bay and Cavite in the Philippines.)

The Alaska stations at Dutch Harbor and Sitka were more easily reached from the West Coast than Hawaii. Dutch Harbor was 2,360nm from Pearl Harbor and 1,970nm from Seattle, while Sitka was 2,900nm from Pearl Harbor and 900nm from Seattle. (In 1941, no overland route to Alaska from the Continental United States existed as the Alaska–Canadian Highway had not yet been built.)

In the event of a war with Japan, even greater distances loomed. The ultimate goal of a campaign against Japan was its Home Islands. They stretched 1,780nm, 40 percent greater than the distance from San Diego, California to Seattle, Washington State. Tokyo Bay, where a peace treaty would be signed after a victorious war, was 3,350nm from Pearl Harbor.

The road to Tokyo was indirect. In 1940–42, it was easy to operate a fleet 1,000–1,500nm from an advance base, especially with underway refueling. It was difficult to nearly impossible when 2,000nm from the nearest place to refuel, rearm, recover and repair. The only factor that permitted US Pacific Fleet operations around Wake was that it was a friendly base.

The Pacific Fleet's route to Tokyo meant controlling first the Marshall Islands and next the Caroline Islands. That was a big leap, especially since those islands had Japanese airfields and aircraft opposition was expected. The Marshalls were 2,000nm distant or more; the nearest, Wotje, was 1,980nm from Pearl Harbor, Jailut was 2,103nm, Kwajalein 2,123nm, and the highly desired Eniwetok 2,360nm. The Carolines were farther still, 2,684nm to Ponape (the nearest) and 3,030nm to Truk. Woleai was even farther from Pearl Harbor than Tokyo, 3,467nm distant. Taking those islands required capturing one of the Marshall Islands and turning it into a forward base. Kwajalein was only 870nm from Truk.

These distances were why fuel oil and diesel fuel were so important. All steamships, the bulk of the US Navy in 1941, burned thick viscous bunker oil. Submarines and a few small warships had diesel engines and used diesel oil, a lighter and more volatile petroleum. Ships burned a lot of oil. A battleship burned between 90 and 150 tons a day steaming at 15 knots. A cruiser burned 40–45 tons a day at that speed and a destroyer 24–25 tons. Fuel consumption increased exponentially with speed. A battleship would double consumption by increasing from 15 to 20 knots. Cruisers and destroyers steaming at 30 knots burned four times the fuel they did at 15 knots.

Since there were a lot of ships, they consumed a lot of oil. Cruising at economical speed, just the nine battleships of the battle line burned 1,000 tons of oil a day. A carrier task force (one carrier accompanied by three to four cruisers and nine destroyers) burned 600 tons at economical speed. Carrier operations often requiring higher speeds would likely burn triple that. In peacetime, with only a quarter of the fleet at sea and economical speeds the norm, the Pacific Fleet would burn 1,000 tons a day in warships alone. That total excludes submarines (which used diesel) and auxiliaries (including fleet oilers). During wartime, it could easily jump to 10,000 tons a day.

Every drop of oil came from the US West Coast on tankers to be stored at Pearl Harbor. The surviving battleships were sent back to the West

The Puget Sound Navy Yard at Bremerton, Washington State was the US Navy's largest West Coast repair facility. It had three dry docks capable of holding battleships and four fitting-out piers. It was the official home port of the battleships. (USNHHC)

Coast once the war began. They used too much oil to idle in Hawaii, drawing down reserves. They remained at the West Coast until need for them arose.

Oil was the most critical logistics issue, but not the only one. Everything except water and fresh food had to be brought to Hawaii. A warship was a small city, ranging from 2,500 men on a carrier to 160 aboard a destroyer. All had to be fed, clothed, housed and provided with everything from laundry service to postage stamps. A battleship's crew went through over 3½ tons of food per day, a carrier's crew 6 tons. Much of this food was preserved. Supplying the Pacific Fleet's personnel in Hawaii and other Pacific bases in 1941 required two medium-size freighters each month to bring the food from the West Coast to Hawaii.

Warships needed ammunition. A battleship carried 100 rounds of main gun ammunition for each main gun and 220 rounds for each 5in. gun, over 900 tons of shells per ship. Cruisers carried 230 tons of ammunition in their magazines. During peacetime, ammunition expenditure was low, limited to practice firing. During combat, it was rapidly expanded. Torpedoes were in short supply, and only 36 were produced each month. Resupply of shells and torpedoes would become critical in combat.

In 1941, the US Pacific Fleet had an excellent collection of naval bases and navy yards to service its needs and a network of naval stations in the Central Pacific. Unfortunately, all but one of its bases (Pearl Harbor in Hawaii) were on the US Pacific Coast. No naval station was capable of supporting any seagoing US Navy warship. Only vessels no larger than destroyers could find a sheltered harbor at a Pacific naval station. The Navy began expanding its shore facilities in 1938, although few expansion projects were complete when 1941 ended.

There were three major West Coast naval bases: Mare Island California; the Puget Sound Naval Yard at Bremerton, Washington; and San Diego Navy

San Diego had been the primary Pacific naval base until the fleet was ordered to Pearl Harbor. A sprawling facility, it had a destroyer base, naval yard, training center and Marine base in addition to the largest naval air station (shown here) on the Pacific Coast. (USNHHC)

Base. Two Navy-controlled ship repair facilities were under construction: the Hunters Point Naval Dry Docks, in San Francisco, California, off San Francisco Bay; and Terminal Island Naval Dry Docks at San Pedro, California, near Los Angeles.

Mare Island was the US Navy's oldest West Coast naval base. Located on a peninsula jutting into San Pablo Bay, it was established shortly after California joined the United States. It was inland, sheltered from attack, yet had easy access to the Pacific through the Golden Gate. Its biggest problem at the start of the 20th century was that its channel was too shallow for battleships.

In addition to its function as a naval base, it was the site of a naval radio station and an important shipbuilding and ship maintenance facility. At the start of 1940, Mare Island had two 883ft dry docks and two building ways. In March 1940, construction began on a fourth dry dock, 435ft by 84ft. In May, a double building way for submarines broke ground. In November, work started on five double ways for ships up to 450ft long.

The Puget Sound Naval Yard was established in 1891. In 1941, it was the only battleship repair facility on the Pacific Coast. Before the 1938 expansion it had three dry docks. All three could hold any Pacific Fleet battleship and two could accommodate Lexington-class carriers, the largest ships in the Pacific Fleet. It had four fitting-out piers which could handle repairs not requiring dry docking. In 1938, construction began on two new dry docks, 997ft by 143ft and 1030ft by 147ft. Both were completed during 1941. Thanks to these facilities, it was considered the home port of the battleships of Battle Force.

San Diego opened in 1922 as a destroyer base, and by 1940 it had grown in importance. In addition to the Naval Destroyer Base, it was home to one of the Pacific Coast's largest naval air stations, headquarters of Amphibious Force, US Pacific Fleet, a US Marine Corps (USMC) Marine Coast base, a USMC training center, and the major communication center on the Pacific Coast. It housed the Naval Radio and Sound Laboratory. It had been the US Pacific Fleet's main port until it moved to Hawaii in 1940.

San Diego had extensive ship repair facilities, primarily intended for ships up to destroyer size. At the start of 1941, it had only *ARD-1*, a 393.5ft-long floating dry dock, capable of carrying a destroyer. In January 1941, a contract was made for a cruiser dry dock capable of carrying one cruiser, three large destroyers or submarines or four smaller destroyers or submarines. Work began in February, but the dock was not complete until April 1942.

The US Navy had two other bases in California: Naval Operating Base, San Francisco and Naval Operating Base, Long Beach. San Francisco included a naval station at Treasure Island, a communications station at San Francisco, a naval air station at Alameda, and Hunters Point Naval Dry Docks. Formerly a civilian yard with two graving docks, it was bought by the Navy in 1940. The Navy was in the process of building four new dry docks there, one 1092ft and three 420ft. Work began in July 1941, but was incomplete at the start of 1942.

Long Beach consisted of a naval air station at Terminal Island, and the Terminal Island Navy Dry Docks, both at San Pedro. Terminal Island had been bought by the Navy in 1938. As at Hunters Point, the Navy Dry Docks were authorized in 1940, with construction beginning in August.

The final US Pacific Fleet naval base was Pearl Harbor, in Oahu. Established in 1899 as a coaling station, it was upgraded to a naval station in 1908. With completion of a dry dock in 1919 it, with Subic Bay and Cavite on Luzon, became the US Navy's only full naval bases outside the United States in the Pacific. A channel was dredged to permit the Navy's biggest warships to enter, although it lacked the capacity to house the entire Pacific Fleet until the mid-1930s. Before that, the fleet anchored at Lahaina Roads off Maui when visiting Hawaii.

In 1939, the navy yard had a 1,002ft by 138ft dry dock with supporting industrial equipment, a marine railway, administrative offices, two above-ground fuel-oil tank farms, a supply depot, and a naval air station on Ford Island which was then shared with the US Army. A submarine base had been built in 1922 and occupied 32 acres. Contracts were let in 1939 to build two new dry docks, a 1,002ft by 147ft battleship dry dock and a 467ft by 104ft destroyer dry dock. The battleship dry dock was completed in November 1941.

Pearl Harbor was the only major US naval base in the Central Pacific. It had dry docks, a massive fuel tank farm, extensive repair facilities and an anchorage capable of housing the entire Pacific Fleet. This shows it in November 1941. (USNHHC)

The Army Air Force shared Ford Island Naval Air Station with the Navy, until Hickam Field on Oahu proper was completed. They moved out between 1939 and 1941. An airship base at Ewa, unused since it was established in 1925, was upgraded to an airfield capable of handling aircraft. In February 1941, it was commissioned as Marine Corps Air Station Ewa. Barber's Point, an outlying field for Ford Island, was also expanded to accommodate the aircraft of two carrier air groups.

Pacific Coast facilities were not part of the US Pacific Fleet. They were operated by Naval Districts independent of the fleets operating out of them. They even had ships (gunboats, destroyers and mine warfare vessels) for coastal frontier defense and yard vessels under their control.

The 11th Naval District covered California south of Point Arguello; the 12th Naval District, California north of Point Arguello; and the 13th Naval District, the Oregon, Washington and Alaska coasts. This included naval stations and naval air stations at Sitka, Kodiak and Dutch Harbor. The Dutch Harbor facilities were still under construction during 1941. These districts also administered US Navy interests in inland states east of the coastal states.

The 14th Naval District covered Hawaii and naval stations in the Central Pacific. It was under the operational control of the US Pacific Fleet. The 15th Naval District was responsible for defense of the Canal Zone and operating the Panama Canal. Its attention was split between the Caribbean and the Pacific.

There were outposts on four outlying Pacific atolls: Wake, Midway, Johnston and Palmyra. Work had begun developing all four after 1938. Before the end of 1941, there was a naval station, a naval air station, and a marine detachment on all four.

Wake was the most forward and strategically important. Two thousand nautical miles from Pearl Harbor and 1,700nm from Tokyo, the Navy considered Wake its most advanced defensible base in the Pacific. Previously uninhabited, Pan American Airlines established a commercial seaplane facility there in 1936. In January 1941, the US Navy began building a seaplane base there capable of operating three patrol squadrons (VPs). A channel was excavated allowing access to the lagoon, fuel tanks were built and facilities added to support the base and its personnel. To protect it, the Navy constructed an airfield and garrisoned Wake with a detachment of the Marine 1st Defense Battalion. A detachment of VMF-211 with 12 F4F3s arrived the first week of December.

Midway, roughly halfway between Wake and Oahu, had hosted the Navy since 1903 when a Navy radio station opened. Pan American built a seaplane base and hotel there in 1936. In 1938, the US began work on a naval station, submarine base and air station at Midway. By 1940, a channel to the lagoon and a seaplane basin were dredged, preparations for a submarine basin began, and a seaplane hangar and facilities for a patrol squadron, and three asphalt-paved runways on Eastern Island were completed. Midway was garrisoned by the Marine 6th Defense Battalion.

Johnston Island, 720nm south-west of Oahu, and Palmyra Island, 960nm south of the Hawaiian Islands, were both coral atolls housing a seaplane base and an airstrip, with channels and docking facilities that could host small warships and auxiliaries. Johnston Island had been used off and on for seaplanes since 1935. Work on permanent facilities on both atolls began in January 1940 and by April 1941 both were garrisoned with detachments of the Marine 1st Defense Battalion. Construction of runways for land-based aircraft began in 1941. They were incomplete by year's end.

COMBAT AND ANALYSIS

The Pacific Fleet's battlefield was the Central Pacific. Japan had been awarded the German-held islands in the Marianas, Caroline and Marshall Islands after World War I. It held these under a League of Nations mandate, and they were collectively known as the Mandate Islands. Japan had bases in all three island chains, which had to be taken before a US advance to the Philippines or Japan could occur. The US held the Hawaiian Islands, several small atolls in the Central Pacific and Guam in the Marianas.

THE FLEET IN COMBAT

When Husband Kimmel took command of the newly-formed Pacific Fleet in February 1941, Japan was at peace with the Western powers (the United States, Britain and the Netherlands) in the Pacific and Far East. His mission was to use the Pacific Fleet to keep Japan from going to war.

On February 2, 1941, Japan had ten battleships, four fleet and four light carriers, 18 heavy and 19 small light cruisers, and 68 modern and 31 older destroyers. Not all of these could be thrown immediately against the US Pacific Fleet. Japan faced Royal Navy and Netherlands Navy warships in the South China and Java seas and the US Asiatic Fleet operating out of the Philippines.

When Kimmel took command, the Pacific Fleet had 12 battleships, four aircraft carriers, 12 heavy and 14 light cruisers (including five superannuated

US Naval Intelligence was unaware that Japan had converted four Mogami-class and two Tone-class light cruisers to heavy cruisers, replacing triple 6in. turrets with twin 8in. turrets. This left the Pacific Fleet badly outnumbered in heavy cruisers. Shown is *Tone*, with twin turrets clearly visible. (USNHHC)

Omaha-class ships), 67 modern and four old destroyers, 18 fleet and six old submarines and 12 fleet oilers. It also had 16 transports which could move two divisions of troops available to it to invade and occupy several of the Japanese-held Marshall Islands within two months of war breaking out.

The US believed the Pacific Fleet was more powerful than the Imperial Navy in every category except aircraft carriers. Only the Japanese 4th Fleet (made up of light cruisers and smaller warships) and the 6th Fleet (with 30 submarines) were in the Mandates. The Imperial Navy's striking power was concentrated in the 1st Fleet, normally stationed in Japan, and the 2nd and 3rd Fleets, operating out of Formosa. The Pacific Fleet's job was to sweep away the 4th Fleet, and lure the other three fleets into the Mandates for battle.

The belief in Pacific Fleet superiority was based on several flawed assumptions. The most important was that the Imperial Navy had only 13 true heavy cruisers, as six of the Imperial Navy's 19 heavy cruisers were originally intended as light cruisers. Japan substituted an 8in. main battery for the 6in. guns they reportedly carried. Additionally, these six "light" cruisers were the only ones equivalent to the nine modern US light cruisers. The rest were training cruisers or pre-Treaty light cruisers, intended as destroyer leaders.

The Office of Naval Intelligence assessment assumed the Imperial Navy remained static during 1941; instead, it was growing. By December 1941, it had added another two fleet carriers, one light cruiser and eight new destroyers to its fleet. It was reorganized late in 1941, with the six fleet carriers withdrawn from their original fleets and placed in the First Carrier Fleet, the *Kidō Butai*. They were joined by two fast battleships, two heavy cruisers and nine destroyers. This went undetected because the ships all remained stationed in the same home harbor.

Kimmel took command while Britain and the United States were holding talks in Washington on a common global approach to the Axis. These talks yielded the ABC-1 Staff Agreement, on March 27, 1941, which shaped the Pacific Fleet's mission for the rest of the year.

It set a "Germany first" policy for any war the United States entered, even if Japan attacked first. Britain and the US would attempt to dissuade Japan from further aggression, to avoid war. Under this agreement, the US Army had responsibility for holding Hawaii, the Canal Zone and the Pacific Coast of North America. It gave the US Pacific Fleet four objectives:

Divert Imperial Navy forces away from the Malay Barrier (protecting the oil-rich Dutch East Indies) through diversionary attacks in the Japanese Mandate Islands.

In May 1941, three battleships, one aircraft carrier, four light cruisers and 18 destroyers, along with three oilers and transports, were transferred from the Pacific Fleet to the Atlantic Fleet. This included the aircraft carrier *Yorktown*, docked at Norfolk in July 1941. (USNHHC)

Support subequatorial British and Commonwealth naval forces to 155 East longitude.

Protect communications between Hawaii and Australia.

Prepare to capture the Marshalls and the Carolines.

The final objective downgraded the amphibious part of the Pacific Fleet's plans. The two divisions assigned to the Pacific Fleet, the Army 3rd Infantry Division and the 2nd Marine Division, remained notionally part of the Pacific Fleet, but were unavailable for landings without clearance from Washington. The 3rd Infantry was earmarked for eventual European commitment. The 2nd Marine was being shifted to the Marine Corps' reserve as elements of the 1st Marine Division were being prepared for operations in the Atlantic.

Given these orders, the offensive-minded Kimmel sought a way to lure the Imperial Navy within striking distance of the Pacific Fleet without exposing the Pacific Fleet to heavy air attack by the Imperial Navy's land-based aircraft. He decided the solution lay in exploiting the planned expansion of Wake. He would use Wake as bait, luring the Japanese fleet to the isolated spot, where the Pacific Fleet could fall on the Japanese beyond the range of most land-based

VPs AT WAKE (overleaf)

Kimmel planned to make Wake Island a forward base. It was simultaneously to serve as a springboard for operations against the northernmost of the Japanese-held Marshall Islands, and bait to lure the Japanese fleet into attacking it, where it could be ambushed.

A key part of the plan was transforming Wake's lagoon into a seaplane base where US Navy reconnaissance squadrons (called VPs, for the Navy code for aViation Patrol squadron) could operate. The Pacific Fleet planned to build facilities for three seaplane squadrons at Wake, clearing coral heads and dredging the lagoon to a depth acceptable for Catalina PBY flying boats.

The effort was simplified as Pan American Airlines had built facilities for its China Clipper airliners to land in the lagoon, including a dock and seaplane ramp. However, the lagoon was too shallow (and too small) to admit seaplane tenders. All supplies for the VPs operating out of Wake had to be lightered from ships anchored offshore, vulnerable to submarines, and then cached on one of the three islands in the atoll. Maintenance facilities were required on the atoll as well, and these were planned but never fully developed.

Regardless, throughout 1941 VP squadrons would be sent to Wake to demonstrate its potential as a base.

They would remain for a limited period – generally a week or two – then return to Hawaii. This plate captures the action in one such exercise on May 25, 1941.

The 12 aircraft of VP11, normally stationed out of NAS Kaneohe on Oahu's east coast, are at Wake, where they conducted reconnaissance, practicing to detect an attempted Japanese invasion of the island. Nine PBY Catalinas are moored on the north side of the lagoon in the first of three squadron anchorages created in the lagoon. A tenth is taking off on a morning patrol. Two other PBYs launched previously are already on patrol. Due to prevailing winds, aircraft always take off and land headed east.

The European situation unraveled Kimmel's plans. The US wanted Britain to send a battleship force to Singapore. It also planned to occupy Iceland to strengthen Roosevelt's Atlantic Neutrality Zone. To support that, the US Navy transferred three battleships, a carrier, four light cruisers and two destroyer flotillas from the Pacific Fleet to the Atlantic Fleet. Accompanying them were three fleet oilers and three transports. By the time the transfer was complete in May 1941, the Pacific Fleet was inferior to the Japanese Navy in every category.

aircraft. (Kimmel was unaware that the A6M Zero fighter and the G3M and G4M could reach Wake from Japanese island bases.) A strong air garrison at Wake could threaten the Marshalls.

Drawing Japanese attention north to Wake would allow more aggressive raiding from the east by Pacific Fleet carriers. This plan violated the spirt of Kimmel's orders to remain on the defensive, but he kept Washington unaware of the forward nature of his plans. Forgiveness would come when he defeated the Imperial Navy.

Japan invaded China in 1937 and had been nibbling away at Chinese-held parts of that country ever since. Following the fall of France in May 1940, the Vichy France government and Japan "negotiated" an agreement allowing Japan to occupy the north-eastern quarter of French Indochina. In July 1941, further Japanese pressure allowed Japan to occupy all of French Indochina. This gave the Imperial Navy use of Camranh Bay and Saigon as a springboard to invade British- and Dutch-held territories abutting the South China Sea. It also flanked defenses in the US-held Philippines.

President Roosevelt, who had previously embargoed scrap iron sales to Japan when it occupied north-eastern Indochina, now banned export of oil to Japan. He convinced Britain and the Netherlands to join the embargo. Japan would get no oil unless it relinquished Indochina.

That left Japan with a six-month reserve of oil unless it complied. Instead of backing down, Japan decided to seize the embargoed resources from their owners unless the embargo was lifted. In 1904, when war loomed between Russia and Japan, the Japanese had opened negotiations with Russia, while preparing for war if diplomacy proved unsatisfactory. It did the same with the United States in 1941. Conducting negotiations in Washington to lift the oil embargo, Japan simultaneously plotted a massive offensive against Britain, the Netherlands and the United States.

In the first half of 1941, Kimmel continued expanding the infrastructure on the island stations, particularly Wake and Midway. The seaplane base at Wake was operational by May, and work had started on the airstrip. Kimmel conducted exercises off Wake in May, including operating a VP squadron from its lagoon. It was still just a remote base, as seaplane tenders could not enter the lagoon safely. There was a narrow boat channel, dredged to a 13ft depth. The seaplane operating area was only 6ft to 10ft deep. With tenders forced to anchor in an open roadstead vulnerable to submarines, maintaining a long-term VP presence during wartime would have been difficult.

By July, it was obvious Japan planned to attack somewhere. The question was where. Not Siberia;

The seaplane base at Wake Island was functioning by May 1941. It operated in Wake's lagoon, with the shore facilities on Peale Island. This picture, taken on May 25, shows seven PBYs moored in the lagoon. A China Clipper is tied up at the Pan American Airlines dock. (USNHHC)

in April, Japan signed a non-aggression pact with the Soviet Union. Given Japan's occupation of Indochina, the obvious answer was south-east into the South China Sea and the resource-rich colonies then held by Britain and the Netherlands.

The nightmare scenario from the standpoint of Pacific Fleet intelligence would be for Japan to confine its attacks to Britain and Dutch holdings, leaving US possessions untouched. That would put the US in the position of declaring war on Japan to protect European colonies. US public opinion might dictate the US would sit out joining any war fought exclusively against European powers. Ignoring the US would leave Japan's line of communications open to attack by a potentially hostile power, yet through October the Pacific Fleet's intelligence was predicting that outcome.

Even in November, when Pacific Fleet intelligence assessments shifted to include a Japanese declaration of war against the US, it was felt that Japanese attacks would be limited to the Philippines and Guam. Guam was defenseless and attacking the Philippines would secure South China Sea lines of communications for Japan. Kimmel hoped rather than expected that Japan would attack Wake.

There was every indication that Japan's major surface units were committed to the South China Sea, not the central Pacific. An attack on Wake by just the weak 4th Fleet (the only Imperial Navy surface force in the Mandates) would be suicidal with the much more powerful Pacific Fleet in Hawaii. In the view of Pacific Fleet intelligence officers, the Pacific Fleet would remain spectators during the war's opening months. With no troops available to invade the Marshalls, all Kimmel could do was trail his coat off Wake and raid the Marshalls. Kimmel had the Pacific Fleet conduct another exercise off Wake in late October.

The one disquieting note as November ended and December began was that intelligence had lost track of the Japanese fleet carriers, now six in number. From a signals intelligence perspective, they had vanished. They seemed to be in Japan's Inland Sea, but that assessment was based on inference.

On December 2, 1941, Kimmel asked the Pacific Fleet's intelligence officer, Lieutenant Commander Edwin Layton, to provide a briefing on assessed Japanese intentions. Kimmel had received a message from the Navy Department advising that Japan was expected to go to war almost immediately and he wanted to know what to expect.

During the briefing, Layton said Japan had a large task force, including transports, off the coast of Indochina and Thailand, adding that there was no trace of Japanese fleet carrier divisions. Traffic analysis had not heard from them since November 25. Kimmel asked: "You mean they [the carriers] could be coming around Diamond Head, and you wouldn't know it?" Layton conceded the point, but added: "I hope they would be sighted before now."

Kimmel took the attack warning seriously. In the first week of December 1941, he sent *Enterprise* to Wake and *Lexington* to Midway to fly off reinforcements

for the air garrisons of those islands. He also attempted to ensure that any Japanese forces approaching Pearl Harbor were sighted before they got close. Catalinas began patrolling the approached to Oahu. They covered an arc from due south to north-west, watching the directions from which Imperial Navy ships could reach Hawaii from Japanese possessions in the Mandates. The seas to the north of Hawaii were skipped as the Japanese would have to cross thousands of miles of storm-tossed ocean to reach striking distance of Hawaii.

However, the *Kidō Butai* was approaching Hawaii from that direction. Little traffic crossed those North Pacific waters, which offered the best route to reach Hawaii undetected. The *Kidō Butai* sortied from Tankan Bay in the Kurile Islands on November 25. As dusk fell on December 6, it was within striking distance of Pearl Harbor.

Battleship Row on the south-east side of Ford Island and the naval air station on Ford Island were the initial Japanese targets during the Pearl Harbor attack. It opened at 0755hrs, with Japanese dive and level bombers hitting Ford Field. Ironically, less than ten years earlier, the US Fleet had practiced its own Sunday morning attack on Pearl Harbor during wargames. That attack was ruled successful. Yet on December 7 it was the last thing anyone expected. Most of Japan's navy was in the South China Sea, and intelligence assumed the carriers were with them, supporting operations planned there. (USNHHC)

With six big fleet aircraft carriers and 423 combat aircraft, the *Kidō Butai* was the largest concentration of carrier air power up to that point in history. It included the four carriers Layton had lost track of, and two others, *Zuikaku* and *Shokaku*, commissioned only months earlier and on their first operation with the Imperial Navy.

Equally ironically, the Inland Sea is where most of the Imperial Navy's commanders, including Admiral Nagumo Chūichi, commanding the *Kidō Butai*, would have preferred them to be. The Pearl Harbor strike was the concept of one man, Admiral Yamamoto Isoroku, who commanded the Imperial Navy's Combined Fleet. He believed a carrier strike at Pearl Harbor could knock out both the US Pacific Fleet and the Pearl Harbor Naval Base, confining the US to the eastern half of the Pacific until both were rebuilt. Yamamoto was so adamantly in favor of the attack that, when his superiors vetoed it he threatened to resign. His prestige was so great they backed down, permitting the attack.

On the morning of December 7, Nagumo sent 353 aircraft towards Oahu. Thirty fighters remained over the carriers on combat air patrol, while 40 others were kept in reserve. Of the strike force, 40 carried torpedoes (specially modified for Pearl Harbor's shallow water), 103 were level bombers, and 131 were dive-bombers, escorted by 79 fighters.

The first Japanese aircraft sighted Oahu at roughly 0740hrs and took another 20 minutes to reach Pearl Harbor. Minutes before reaching the naval base, Japanese fighters and bombers were attacking the Army's Wheeler Field and Marine Air Station Ewa. A few others peeled off to attack Naval Air Station Kaneohe on Oahu's east side. Bombs started dropping on Pearl Harbor at 0755hrs, when Ford Island was attacked.

The crews aboard ships were just waking up for duty. "Colors," the flag-raising ceremony, was held at 0800hrs. The ready signal for colors had been signaled at 0755hrs, and ships were awaiting it. Most men were preparing for Sunday inspection held later that day. Due to heightened security, all ships were at Condition 3, able to keep systems manned and operating and ready to communicate. Weapons and magazines were unmanned and boilers were cold on most ships moored in harbor. Ready ammunition for machine guns was in locked boxes. Many of the officers with the keys were ashore.

A minute after the first bombs hit Ford Island, Rear Admiral W. R. Furlong, the Senior Officer Present Afloat, hoisted the signal "All ships in harbor sortie" from his flagship, the minelayer *Oglala*. At 0758hrs, Rear Admiral Patrick Bellinger at his Ford Island headquarters radioed "Air Raid, Pearl Harbor – This is no drill." Ships went hastily to General Quarters. Guns and magazines were manned, ready ammunition boxes broken open.

Most ships defiantly continued their flag-raising ceremonies, even as their antiaircraft guns began engaging the attacking aircraft. Firemen fired the ships boilers and prepared to start engines. Some ships began firing back within minutes; within 20 minutes most ships in harbor were shooting; within 30 minutes every ship had opened fire.

Yet that first 15 minutes proved critical. Battleships *West Virginia*, *Arizona*, *Oklahoma* and *California* were moored on Battleship Row, on the south side of Ford Island. All received enough damage to sink them between 0800hrs and 0815hrs. *Tennessee* and *Maryland*, moored between Ford Island and an outboard battleship protected from the torpedoes that tore the other four battleships apart, were hit by bombs.

Only the dry-docked *Pennsylvania* was overlooked in the initial attacks. *Nevada*, hit by just one torpedo, managed to raise steam and got under way by 0840hrs. That attracted the attention of every Japanese aircraft around. *Nevada* took five bomb hits and was forced to beach.

It was no better elsewhere in the harbor. Moored on the north side of Ford Island, where the carriers routinely anchored, was the target ship *Utah*, the old light cruisers *Raleigh* and *Detroit* and seaplane tender *Tangier*. *Utah* (perhaps mistaken for an aircraft carrier) and *Raleigh* were torpedoed, *Utah* sunk.

At the Naval Yard, across the south channel from Battleship Row, the Japanese opened their attack by torpedoing light cruiser *Helena*.

The battleship *Nevada* raised steam during the attack. Casting off its moorings at 0825hrs, it went down the East Channel. The moving battleship drew the attention of Japanese aircraft targeting the Navy Yard. They switched to *Nevada*, leaving the Navy Yard largely undamaged. (USNHHC)

The seaplane tender *Tangier* embarked Marines on December 15 to reinforce Wake's garrison as part of a relief expedition. The expedition did not leave Pearl Harbor until December 17, and by the time it arrived near Wake the garrison had surrendered. (USNHHC)

The torpedo ran under the minelayer *Oglala* to hit the deeper-draft cruiser and flooded *Helena*'s engine room, but flooding was contained and power restored using auxiliary generators. *Oglala* was less lucky. The torpedo blast opened seams in its hull. The subsequent flooding capsized *Oglala* and, never directly hit, its crew later claimed it was "frightened to death."

The Japanese second wave arrived an hour after the first, heading for the repair yards. While a number of those aircraft attacked *Nevada* instead, the rest worked over the repair facilities. Destroyer *Shaw* was hit by a bomb that blew its bow off and sank the floating dry dock. *Pennsylvania*, along with destroyers *Cassin* and *Downes*, were in the Number 1 dry dock. A Japanese bomber landed an incendiary bomb between the two destroyers, which ignited oil that leaked into the dry dock and the subsequent fires consumed both destroyers. *Pennsylvania* was hit by a bomb that did minor damage.

Japanese aircraft also strafed ships throughout the harbor, causing minor damage and casualties. Seaplane tender *Curtiss* was struck by an aircraft it shot down and then hit by a bomb during the second wave. So was destroyer tender *Dobbins*, which was attacked by dive-bombers, along with the four destroyers nested to it. But the US was striking back. Although the first wave got through almost undamaged, the second wave met a wall of antiaircraft fire.

The Japanese also attacked the airfields around Oahu, causing significant damage. The Army's Wheeler, Bellows and Hickam Fields were taken out in the first attack. The aircraft on the ground were easy targets, lined up wingtip-to-wingtip as a precaution against sabotage. Over a quarter of the Army's aircraft were destroyed and only Haleiwa Field, a small satellite field, was overlooked. Haleiwa launched five fighters starting at 0815hrs, but Bellows aircraft stayed on the ground until 0950hrs and Hickam failed to sortie any fighters until 1127hrs. The Haleiwa aircraft claimed five kills at the cost of one loss.

Pacific Fleet airfields fared no better. Ford Field lost half its aircraft in the first minutes of the attack. Ewa Marine Air Station had 33 of the 49 aircraft knocked out by waves of strafing Zero fighters. Worst hit was Kaneohe, where 36 Catalinas were stationed. Three were on patrol, and of those at the base when attacked, 27 were destroyed and six badly damaged. The Pacific Fleet's patrol capabilities were crippled.

After the second wave ended, Admiral Nagumo, a long way from Japan, decided to head home before the US carriers appeared. Despite his subordinates' urgings, by noon the *Kidō Butai* was heading west.

The Pacific Fleet largely sat out the rest of the year, while the real action took place in the South China Sea. The Pacific Fleet had to protect Hawaii and the lines of communications between the West Coast and Australia, which meant holding Midway, Johnston, Palmyra and Canton Atolls. The Japanese were moving into the Gilberts and threatening the Australian route.

Wake, outside that defensive perimeter, changed from acting as bait to attract the Imperial Navy to becoming a trap for its garrison. Japan needed to take it to prevent the US from using it as a base against Japan. It began bombing the base on December 8, and launched an invasion of it on December 11 with ships from the 4th Fleet. Since Japan could not be strong everywhere, the invasion force was small: a light cruiser, two destroyers converted to fast transports and 450 special naval landing force troops – Japan's equivalent of the US Marine Corps.

That force proved inadequate and was driven off. For the next ten days, Wake Island was the Pacific Fleet's focus. Had it been immediately reinforced and vigorously defended it might have been held. The Pacific Fleet, even after Pearl Harbor, was vastly more powerful than the 4th Fleet and available Japanese forces. Kimmel began assembling a strike force centered on just *Saratoga* instead of sending all three carriers together. The other two carriers were given diversionary or supporting roles. Kimmel also gave command of the *Saratoga* task force to a surface officer instead of the carrier-experienced flag officer aboard *Saratoga*.

BUFFALO RUN (overleaf)

The last tragic act of 1941 was played out at Wake Island. The first Japanese attempt to capture Wake was driven off on December 11, 1941. The Pacific Fleet mounted a relief expedition which included more ammunition and a Marine reinforcement, both ground troops and more aircraft. Aboard *Saratoga*, the aircraft carrier in the relief force, were 18 Buffaloes of Marine fighter squadron VFM-221. They were to replace the 12 Wildcats of VFM-211, lost repelling the first invasion.

Organizational confusion delayed its departure until December 14, and there were further delays when rough seas meant destroyers could not be refueled. At 0800hrs on December 23, the task force sent was 425nm from Wake, close enough to fly the 18 VFM-221 Buffaloes to island, but by then it was too late. The Japanese had made a second set of landings at 0235hrs, and at 0500hrs Commander Winfield Scott Cunningham, who commanded Wake's garrison, signaled: "The enemy is on the island. The issue is in doubt." As a result, Admiral William Pye, temporarily commanding the Pacific Fleet, ordered the recall of the relief force as the Marine pilots awaited orders to launch their aircraft and relieve their comrades on Wake.

There was no launch that day and the task force returned to Pearl Harbor. Wake's loss left Midway the Pacific Fleet's westernmost outpost, and the Buffaloes of VFM-221 were diverted there. On Christmas Day, as the task force passed Midway, 14 Buffaloes departed *Saratoga* for Midway and became part of the air garrison there. This plate shows the Buffaloes as they begin their takeoff run for Midway – and a rendezvous with destiny at the Battle of Midway in June 1942.

The leading aircraft has started its takeoff run, its tail lifted off but its wheels still on deck. The other pilots wait their turn, while sailors on the flight deck make final preparations. At the stern of the flight deck are three SBD Dauntlesses from *Saratoga*'s scouting squadron, waiting to relieve other aircraft.

Departure from Pearl Harbor was delayed until December 14. The other task forces ended up chasing phantoms in other parts of the Central Pacific. More time was wasted refueling the destroyers as *Saratoga* neared Wake. *Saratoga* was still a day short of reaching Wake on the evening of December 22. Meanwhile, the Japanese were launching a second invasion attempt. This one was reinforced to 2,000 troops accompanied by four heavy and three light cruisers. Also, two carriers left the *Kidō Butai* to provide air support.

The second landing took place on December 22 (Hawaii time; Wake was on the other side of the International Date Line). Kimmel had been relieved on December 17 and the cautious Admiral Pye was in charge until Kimmel's replacement, Chester Nimitz, arrived. The report that carrier aircraft were attacking Wake led Pye to order the withdrawal of the *Saratoga* force, and Wake fell later that day.

ANALYSIS

On December 17, 1941, ten days after the attack on Pearl Harbor, Husband Kimmel was relieved of command of the US Pacific Fleet, and Rear Admiral Chester A. Nimitz was appointed its commander. It was a full admiral's command, and, as with Kimmel in February 1941, assuming this rank promoted Nimitz over more senior admirals.

Like Kimmel, Nimitz was viewed as the right man for the job, and it was a judgment his record would demonstrate correct. He proved the most brilliant strategic naval commander of World War II and one of the top ten in history. Japan did itself no favors by forcing the replacement of the unimaginative and conventional Kimmel with the far more capable Nimitz.

Nimitz was in Washington, where he was Chief of the US Navy's Bureau of Navigation, and he did not arrive in Hawaii until Christmas Day. He spent a few days orienting himself to conditions, keeping most of Kimmel's staff and bringing only his flag secretary with him from Washington. He assumed command in a change-of-command ceremony held on December 31, 1941. Traditionally, the ceremony was held aboard ship, usually a battleship, but every battleship in Pearl Harbor was either damaged or sunk.

Nimitz held the change-of-command ceremony aboard the submarine *Grayling*, saying afterwards that the Japanese attack left no other deck

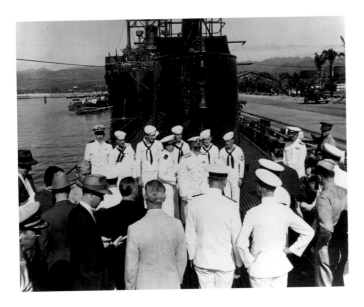

On December 31, 1941, Chester Nimitz read himself into command of the US Pacific Fleet on the deck of *Grayling*, a fleet submarine. This sent an important symbolic message, that carriers and submarines had displaced battleships as the Pacific Fleet's main offensive weapons. (USNHHC)

available, but he chose *Grayling* for a different reason: he had commanded submarines before, during and immediately after World War I.

Six hours after the attack on Pearl Harbor, the Navy Department in Washington messaged the Commander, Submarine Force, US Pacific Fleet: "Execute unrestricted air and submarine warfare against Japan." Nimitz endorsed that message, and the ceremony aboard *Grayling* underscored that endorsement. The 1941 Pacific Fleet was gone, replaced by a new one where submarines and aircraft carriers were the primary offensive weapon of the Pacific Fleet.

December 7 left five battleships, a target ship, a minelayer, a repair ship, a tug and *YFD-2* resting on the bottom of Pearl Harbor. Three other battleships were damaged by bombs, two light cruisers had been torpedoed, two destroyers completely wrecked, two others damaged and a seaplane tender damaged by bombs. There were also 2,403 dead, missing or mortally wounded, and 1,178 wounded. Most were from the Navy, including 1,177 from *Arizona* alone.

Two of the sunken battleships never returned to duty. One was destroyed beyond repair. A second was unneeded by the time it was refloated. The rest of the battleships were patched up and returned to service, some as soon as January 1942. So were the various cruisers, destroyers and auxiliaries damaged that day. Two destroyers, *Cassin* and *Downes*, should have been written off as constructive total losses, but instead, to deny Japan credit for their destruction, were rebuilt at greater effort than if they had been replaced by two new ships. *Utah* and *Arizona* were left in place.

Absent the loss of life, Pearl Harbor did not significantly degrade the capabilities of the US Pacific Fleet. Pearl Harbor's tank farm was not attacked. Had this been destroyed, the Pacific Fleet would have had to withdraw to the Pacific Coast until the tanks were repaired and refilled. Nor were the repair facilities really damaged. A handful of bombs fell on them, mainly aimed at the ships within the facilities. Communications facilities, workshops, and offices were overlooked. The submarine base was completely ignored.

By sidelining the battleships, the Japanese attack created a more effective Pacific Fleet. With most of its battle line on the bottom of Pearl Harbor, the Pacific Fleet was forced to focus on its carriers, the decisive weapon of the Pacific War. It aborted the planned battleship sortie to Wake Island, something that would have failed in its goal to lure the Japanese battleships or even its carriers to oppose them.

The bulk of the Imperial Navy's surface force, including its battleships and heavy cruisers, would have remained in the South China Sea to support landings on territories skirting that sea – Malaya, the Dutch East Indies and the Philippines. The Imperial Navy would have shifted torpedo-carrying twin-engine land-based attack bombers (known as *rikko*) to their airfields around Wake. These would have dealt with the Pacific Fleet's Battle Force in the same way they dealt with *Prince of Wales* and *Repulse* off the coast of Malaya.

The battleships would have been sent to the bottom in water too deep to refloat them, with much higher casualties.

That assumes Kimmel actually *sent* Battle Force to defend Wake or raid the Marshalls. War has a way of making commanders reconsider their plans. The US Navy knew what aircraft were capable of doing to warships.

If Yamamoto had been overridden, the carriers used by the *Kidō Butai* committed to the South China Sea and Pearl Harbor left unmolested, the US would still have gone to war with Japan on December 8. Japanese plans included attacking the Philippines, Guam and Wake, US possessions. The fleet almost certainly would have taken a few days after a declaration of war to sail. Aircraft carriers *Lexington* and *Enterprise* were at sea on December 7. Kimmel would have wanted the air cover they provided. He would have waited for them to arrive, refuel and re-provision before sending the Pacific Fleet to Wake.

Prince of Wales and *Repulse* were sunk by *rikko* aircraft on December 9 (Hawaii time, east of the International Date Line). It took six days for battleships to steam from Oahu to Wake, longer if accompanied by fleet oilers. Even had the Pacific Fleet left Pearl Harbor on December 8, Kimmel – or his superior, Chief of Naval Operations Harold Stark – would have several days to digest the implications of the sinking of *Prince of Wales* and *Repulse*.

Risking battleships to lure out Imperial Navy heavy units, especially their battleships and carriers, could be worth it. Risking them against twin-engine bombers was not. The battleships would have been withdrawn to Pearl Harbor or carefully kept out of range of Japanese aircraft. Wake's relief would have been left to Scouting Force's faster carriers and cruisers. Because battleships were fuel hogs and too slow for the fast naval war being fought in the Pacific, they would likely have spent 1942 where the surviving Pacific Fleet battleship actually spent that year: on the Pacific Coast.

The Pacific Fleet's real weakness was not over-reliance on battleships. It was a flawed aircraft carrier policy. Pacific Fleet carrier task forces throughout 1941 operated with one carrier per task force. Through the first half of 1942 its carrier task forces fielded a maximum of two carriers. As the *Kidō Butai* demonstrated, massing aircraft carriers increased aircraft effectiveness not linearly but multiplicatively or exponentially. Yet up until the creation of the *Kidō Butai* in November 1941 no navy massed carriers. Prior to that, except on very rare occasions, carriers of all nations were sent out individually or possibly in pairs.

In the aftermath of Pearl Harbor, *Yorktown* and *Hornet* were rushed to the Pacific. Yet even with five carriers in the Pacific, these carriers never operated as a single group during 1942. Even at Midway, the three carriers were organized into two independent task forces. It took the hard lesson of battle to teach the Pacific Fleet the necessity of massing carriers. Yet war losses and battle damage kept the carriers in one or two carrier forces until October 1943.

Despite its spectacular defeat at Pearl Harbor, the 1941 US Pacific Fleet was better prepared for a naval war in the Pacific than its Imperial Navy opponent. The Japanese held superiority in aircraft quality, torpedoes and night-fighting capabilities in 1941 and early 1942. The Pacific Fleet better understood the role logistics and maintenance would play in a naval war spanning hemispheric distances.

Japan, given a choice between destroying warships or infrastructure at Pearl Harbor, chose warships. In the immediate aftermath of the December 7 attack, Pearl Harbor concentrated on fixing the damaged facilities. Refloating *YFD-2*, opening Dry Dock No. 2 and clearing Dry Dock No. 1 of the wreckage of *Cassin* and *Downes* (and extracting *Pennsylvania* from the dry dock) took the highest priority.

The Pacific Fleet that won the Pacific War was different from the 1941 Pacific Fleet, which was the last US battleship fleet. As explained earlier, this was due less to a belief in the supremacy of the battleship than recognition that circumstances forced the Pacific Fleet to lead with battleships. A more imaginative commander than Kimmel might have found different solutions.

Nimitz's concept of calculated risk, which permitted an inferior force to attack a superior force if the potential gain justified the loss risked, was an example. It liberated fleet commanders from Alfred Thayer Mahan's insistence on guaranteed superiority before engaging in combat. Nimitz used it to great advantage, most notably at Midway. It was outside-the-box thinking. Was it forced on Nimitz by Pearl Harbor? Possibly, but possibly not.

Even by 1941, the carriers had been unchained from the battleships, operating independently of the battle line through much of the year. Kimmel's plans to use the carriers to raid the Marshalls were echoed by Nimitz in the raids Nimitz ordered in February 1942. Admittedly, Kimmel planned to use the raids to lure the Japanese to the battle line, but both operations used the carriers independently.

The Pacific Fleet of 1942–45 was built on the foundation laid by the 1941 Pacific Fleet. The 1941 Pacific Fleet planned a march across the Pacific and prepared to execute that march. It practiced underway refueling extensively, and planned ways to throw up sophisticated advance bases. Ulithi, set up in 1944, was the ultimate culmination of that planning, but it was not unique. Once peacetime spending restrictions were lifted, the US Navy built bases throughout the Pacific that let their warships carry the war to the enemy.

Destroying Pearl Harbor's tank farm and repair facilities would have forced the Pacific Fleet to the North American West Coast. All fuel was stored in unprotected above-ground tanks, and the tanks and stored fuel could easily have been destroyed with a handful of aircraft. (USNHHC)

FURTHER READING

My goal in this book was to describe the 1941 Pacific Fleet. I started on February 2, 1941 when the fleet was created and ended on December 31. This covered the period when Husband Kimmel commanded until he was formally relieved by Chester Nimitz. The US Pacific Fleet of January 2, 1942 was fundamentally different from the fleet of February 2, 1941. What I attempt to do is explain why they were different. This book looks at the Pacific Fleet's structure, organization and behavior in 1941 and shows how they created the 1942 fleet.

I tried to look at circumstances from the perspective of the participants at the time of the events. Hindsight is 20:20, more difficult is determining why rational and highly professional men made decisions that seem obviously wrong today. My research revealed several surprises. US Navy admirals were not nearly as wedded to battleships as current conventional wisdom holds, and even the carrier advocates were then unaware of the power of massed carriers.

The sources listed below represent the major references I used to write this book. Edward Miller's *War Plan Orange* is probably the best starting point to put someone in the mindset of the prewar admirals. I also recommend the following websites:

http://www.niehorster.org/013_usa/_41_usn/_usn.html and http://www.niehorster.org/014_japan/41-12-08_navy/_ijn.html (for the 1941 USN and IJN orders of battle)

http://navweaps.com/ (for details on weapons)

https://www.navsource.org/ (a useful photo site, but even more useful as a source of information on the ships)

References marked with an * are available online.

Blair, Clay Jr., *Silent Victory: The US Submarine War Against Japan*, J. B. Lippincott Company, New York and Philadelphia (1975)

Carlson, Elliot, *Joe Rochefort's War: The Odyssey of the Codebreaker Who Outwitted Yamamoto at Midway*, Naval Institute Press, Annapolis, Maryland (2011)

Carter, Worrall Reed, *Beans, Bullets, and Black Oil: The Story of Fleet Logistics Afloat in the Pacific During World War II*, Department of the Navy, Washington DC (1953)*

Cheasneau, Roger, *Aircraft Carriers of the World, 1914 to the Present: An Illustrated Encyclopedia*, Arms and Armour Press, London (1984)

Commander, Aircraft Battle Force, *Current Tactical Orders and Doctrine: US Fleet Aircraft*, Vol. 1 (Carrier Aircraft) and Vol. 3 (Patrol Aircraft), Naval Air Station, Pearl Harbor (1941)

Friedman, Norman, *Naval Radar*, Naval Institute Press, Annapolis, Maryland (1981), Naval Institute Press, Annapolis, Maryland (1984)

Friedman, Norman, *US Cruisers: An Illustrated History*, Naval Institute Press, Annapolis, Maryland (1984)

Friedman, Norman, *US Destroyers: An Illustrated History*, Naval Institute Press, Annapolis, Maryland (1989)

McMurtrie, Francis E., editor, *Jane's Fighting Ships, 1942*, The MacMillan Company, New York (1943)

Miller, Edward S., *War Plan Orange: The US Strategy to Defeat Japan*, Naval Institute Press, Annapolis, Maryland (1991)

Morison, Samuel Eliot, *History of United States Naval Operations in World War II, Vol. 3: The Rising Sun in the Pacific*, Little, Brown, Boston, Massachusetts (1946)

Sayers, Ken W., *U.S. Navy Auxiliary Vessels: A History and Directory from World War I to Today*, McFarland and Company, Jefferson, North Carolina (2019)

United States Bureau of Yards and Docks, *Building the Navy's Bases: History of the Bureau of Yards and Docks and the Civil Engineer Corps, Vol. 1 and 2*, United States Government Printing Office, Washington DC (1947)*

Mechanics assemble an F4F3 Wildcat on *Enterprise*'s hangar deck. Spare aircraft are tied to the hangar overhead, including a Devastator and a Dauntless. All aircraft have markings for other carriers, and *Enterprise* might be ferrying the aircraft to those carriers. This picture was taken October 28, 1941. (USNHHC)

INDEX

References to images are in **bold**.

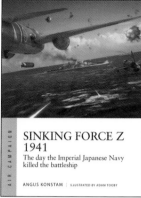
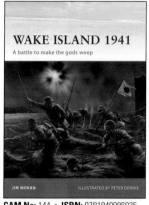
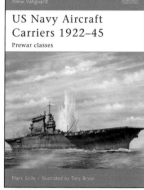
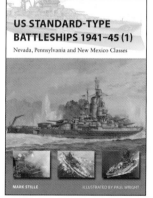
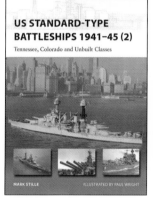

US NAVY PACIFIC FLEET 1941

America's mighty last battleship fleet

INCLUDES:
- Detailed original artwork
- 3D diagrams and maps
- Expert analysis

When the Japanese attacked Pearl Harbor, the Pacific Fleet was the most powerful in the US Navy. It was still dominated by battleships, but had been developing naval aviation since the late 1930s and integrating it with the fleet's battleship-led doctrine.

This book is the first to examine the Pacific Fleet as it was intended to fight, and how it had been training and preparing in the months leading up to December 7, 1941. Naval historian Mark Lardas explains how, contrary to modern assumptions, the fleet was not wedded to the battleship, but was hedging its bets, building up both its carrier and battleship strength. Most crucially, it had also been developing and honing a massive fleet train, allowing it to operate easily thousands of miles from home. It was this foundation that enabled the Pacific Fleet to adapt so rapidly to the new world of carrier-led naval warfare, and first check and then defeat the Imperial Japanese Navy.

With superb artwork, archive photos and 3D diagrams, this is a portrait of the Pacific Fleet during 1941, the last time and place when battleship doctrine held sway.

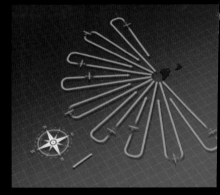

OSPREY PUBLISHING

ISBN 978-1-4728-5950-1

9 781472 859501

52300

www.ospreypublishing.com

US $23.00 | UK £15.99 | CAN $31.00

OSPREY
PUBLISHING

CHROME DOME 1960–68

The B-52s' high-stakes Cold War nuclear operation

PETER E. DAVIES | ILLUSTRATED BY ADAM TOOBY

Author

Peter E. Davies has written or co-written more than 20 books on modern American combat aircraft, including the standard reference work on US Navy and Marine Corps Phantom II operations, *Gray Ghosts*. He is also a contributor to *Aeroplane Monthly*, *Aviation News*, and *Aircraft Illustrated*. He is based in Bristol, UK.

Illustrator

Adam Tooby is an internationally renowned digital aviation artist and illustrator. His work can be found in publications worldwide and as box art for model aircraft kits. He also runs a successful illustration studio and aviation prints business. He is based in Cheshire, UK.

Other titles in the series

ROLLING THUNDER 1965–68
Johnson's air war over Vietnam

RICHARD P. HALLION | ILLUSTRATED BY ADAM TOOBY

ACM No: 3 • **ISBN:** 9781472823205

OPERATION *LINEBACKER II* 1972
The B-52s are sent to Hanoi

MARSHALL L. MICHEL III | ILLUSTRATED BY JIM LAURIER

ACM No: 6 • **ISBN:** 9781472827609

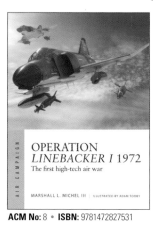

OPERATION *LINEBACKER I* 1972
The first high-tech air war

MARSHALL L. MICHEL III | ILLUSTRATED BY ADAM TOOBY

ACM No: 8 • **ISBN:** 9781472827531

HO CHI MINH TRAIL 1964–73
Steel Tiger, *Barrel Roll*, and the secret air wars in Vietnam and Laos

PETER E. DAVIES | ILLUSTRATED BY ADAM TOOBY

ACM No: 18 • **ISBN:** 9781472842534

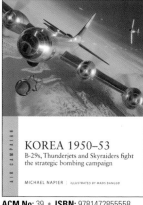

KOREA 1950–53
B-29s, Thunderjets and Skyraiders fight the strategic bombing campaign

MICHAEL NAPIER | ILLUSTRATED BY MADS BANGSØ

ACM No: 39 • **ISBN:** 9781472855558

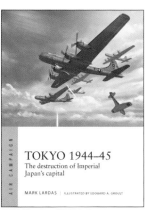

TOKYO 1944–45
The destruction of Imperial Japan's capital

MARK LARDAS | ILLUSTRATED BY EDOUARD A. GROULT

ACM No: 40 • **ISBN:** 9781472860354